READING THE GOSPEL OF MARK AS A NOVEL

Reading the
Gospel of Mark as a Novel

GEERT VAN OYEN

translated by
Leslie Robert Keylock

CASCADE *Books* • Eugene, Oregon

READING THE GOSPEL OF MARK AS A NOVEL

Cascade Books
An Imprint of Wipf and Stock Publishers
199 W. 8th Ave., Suite 3
Eugene, OR 97401

www.wipfandstock.com

ISBN 13: 978-1-4982-2219-8

Cataloging-in-Publication data:

Van Oyen, Geert

Reading the Gospel of Mark as a novel / Geert Van Oyen; translated by Leslie Robert Keylock

x + 144 p. ; 23 cm. —Includes bibliographical references.

ISBN 13: 978-1-4982-2219-8

1. Bible—Hermeneutics. 2. Bible. Mark—Criticism, Narrative. I. Title.

BS2585.52 V25 2014

Manufactured in the U.S.A.

Contents

Preface ix

FIRST PART: READING THE BIBLE TODAY

1. **Mark: An Enigmatic "Novel"** 3
   Reading a Book of the Bible as a Novel 3
   What's New? 4
   A Coded Message in Mark? 5
   An Open Secret 7
   What Can We Expect? 10

2. **An Antivirus Program for the Bible** 12
   A Book Eaten by Moths 12
   Positive Signs, But . . . 13
   Where Do We Read the Bible? The Academic Setting 14
   Where Do We Read the Bible? In the Church 15
   Between Church and University 16
   Why the Gospel of Mark? 18
   A New Program: Reading from the Perspective of Today's Reader 19
   The Evangelist's Intention and the Reader's Interpretation 22
   For Whom and from Whom Is the Gospel? 23

3. **Before Reading: Eliminate the Misunderstandings** 27
   Introduction 27
   The Bible Is Not "True" 29
   To Read the Bible You Have to Be a Believer in the Church 32
   The True Meaning Is Hidden 33
   Conclusion 35
   Structure of Mark's Gospel 36

SECOND PART: MARK'S GOSPEL

4. How Does the Evangelist Narrate? 43
Introduction 43
The "How" of a Narrative 45
Promise and Fulfillment 52
Doublets in the Gospel 55
Summaries 60
Other Stylistic Characteristics 63
Considerations about the Evangelist's Rhetoric 64

5. Jesus with a Question Mark
Reading in Reality 68
The Exegete as a Guide, the Text and the Reader 70
The First Experience of Reading: Under a Flood of Questions 71
First Question: A Demon 71
Second Question: The Scribes 74
More Questions and Criticism from His Enemies 76
Not to Generalize 78
Beating of a Butterfly's Wings 80
But What Is a Gospel? 81
Once Again: Reading in Reality 82

6. The Burden of Honorary Titles 86
Introduction 86
Jesus and His Honorary Titles 87
Son of God 88
Son of God and the Dynamic of Reading 89
Son of God: The Hellenistic Context 91
Son of God: Canvas of the Jewish Background 93
Why Is Jesus So Specific? 94
The Christ 96
The Other Titles 96
The Secret 98

7. The Disciples and Jesus 101
The First Choice 102
Presence 104
The Larger Circle of Jesus' Disciples 105

Failure to Understand Jesus' Words 106
A Question of Perspective 108
Failure to Understand Jesus' Actions 110
The Triangle: Jesus—Disciples—Readers 111
A Hinge Moment: Jesus' Question 114
Jesus' Criteria Concerning the Kingdom of God 115
To Be Continued 117

8. The Strength of Powerlessness 119
Introduction 119
Jesus, God, and Suffering 120
Jesus Dies Alone 122
Jesus' Life and Death Are Well Matched 125
Jesus: The Reader's Revolutionary View of God 127
The Hermeneutic of Golgotha and the Readers 128
The Paradoxical Message of Mark for the Reader 129
What Does "Save Your Life" Mean? 129

9. Epilogue: Where Is Jesus? 132
God's Answer 132
The End of the Narrative and the Reader 133
The Women in Mark 16:1–8 *and the Reader* 135
Jesus, the Crucified, Resurrected One 137
Jesus, the Absent One Present 138
Once Again: The Real Reader 139
To Believe and Not to Believe 141

Preface

Dear reader,

The book you have in your hands is an answer to the author's desire to make known the current state of the exegesis of the Gospel of Mark outside the scholarly universe of the specialists in biblical sciences. It is composed of two main parts. The first explains why it is important today to read the Bible in a different way than the way it has been for long centuries, more precisely since the critical exegesis of the seventeenth century. To be brief: it is less a matter of being informed through the Bible than of letting yourself be transformed by it. It is only when the Bible touches the readers in their personal lives that the text receives all its meaning. So if we can realize this meeting between the text and the readers, the narrative method can be an excellent guide. In the second part, readers are invited to begin the dialogue with the text of the Gospel of Mark. Through the slant of different narrative characteristics of the account, we discover how Mark's author masters the art of attributing an active part to the reader when giving meaning to the text. This is precisely the discovery that we propose from recent exegetical research: it belongs to the readers to invest themselves actively in order to spell out the meaning of the text.

The term "reader" moreover perhaps seems a bit too general. It could stir up the question of knowing whether the present book is really directed to you. You would perhaps be right to think that you have already read so many books on Mark that you have nothing new to discover. Or on the other hand that you have never read anything on Mark and that it cannot be useful to you to begin now. Now, there is no other way to know than taking the risk and to set yourself to reading. The only condition to fulfill amounts in fact to a certain candor. In the role of reader acquainted with the Gospel of Mark, I am forced on my side to place myself in a vulnerable position to the reader who has no malice. We live in a time when the church and society face very grave crises that break what remains of confidence and of certitude among our contemporaries. From that moment it is even more important to go back to the texts that are the source of our tradition, abandoning all the ballast of the past to rediscover in this way the freshness and the energy of the originals. The purpose of this book is thus that once it has been read, readers will begin among them a dialogue on this Gospel of Mark.

Given the conception of this book, I do not wish to burden it with footnotes in a scholarly way. For the same reason I have chosen not to interact with colleagues in the same discipline: there are many specific conventions and specialist journals for those who are interested in others' views. However, the reader who is a bit interested will find at the end of each of the chapters a modest bibliography of a few books to consult whose authors are usually mentioned in the course of the preceding chapter. It goes without saying that there are many more things to say or to write on Mark that this little book does not contain. I think for example of the suffering theme or yet again of the so-called "minor characters." But I have tried to mention here basic things I have learned from the rich contacts at numerous conferences and addresses held for various groups. The auditors have more than once insisted that I put the spoken word into writing. Gospel quotations have been taken from the New Revised Standard Version.

Geert Van Oyen

FIRST PART
Reading the Bible Today

1

Mark: An Enigmatic "Novel"

Reading a Book of the Bible as a Novel

THIS BOOK SPEAKS OF another book, the Gospel of Mark. Whereas the volume of scholarly publications on this Gospel is already incalculable, exegetes continue to produce dozens of books and articles every month. From the moment when a person thinks of writing an umpteenth book on Mark, it is appropriate to first show how it will be new. As for me, I began my research on the earliest of the Gospels in 1985 and my greatest discovery in these almost thirty years has nothing of the sensational and will therefore never end up in a journal. I have not discovered at the end an ancient parchment throwing a completely new light on Jesus and unmasking the Gospels as false! I have not discovered a spectacular insight into Jesus, capable of starting a revolution among believers or undermining their faith! The book does not contain any secret decipherable by a few rare initiates and hidden to everyone else. It nevertheless seemed to me that, in spite of the fact that almost every word of this text can engender long discussions among scholars of the Bible, you do not need to be a specialist to understand what this book is all about. In brief, nothing sensational.

But what brought about these long years of research? Certainly, the Gospel of Mark is not fiction. But in trying to summarize, I believe I have learned that the more one reads the Gospel of Mark as a novel, the more the potential of meaning rises up from the text so that the number of people capable of being touched by the text becomes important. Reading the Gospel as a novel? But is it really allowed? Doesn't it lack respect for a book that is part of the Holy Scriptures? The books of the Bible are not novels, after all! "They are the Word of God," believers will say. "They are interesting historical documents," historians of religion will say. Let us come back to these assertions later. I want to limit myself here to the first approach of the thesis according to which a plurality of meanings of a text can arise. This eventuality does not please everybody. It is much more comfortable to think that a text can only have a single meaning. Moreover, it is what we think most often, because we are convinced of the numerous advantages it presents. Thus, some cling from their ecclesiastical tradition to a slavish reading that gives them the feeling of being in a known territory: everything that is in the text has truly happened and it is not good or even allowable to doubt it; and even if everything does not arise from historical truth, the content is locked up with certitude, solid bases allowing them to erect an indisputable dogma of their faith. In imagining the truth of Gospel in this way, they probably create a world of certainties, but they risk being no longer able to enter into dialogue with more critical and nevertheless also believing readers.

Others swear only by a very precise exegetical method. They hope, for example, to discover Mark's intentions by rebuilding a certain historical situation that could have led the evangelist to write his book. But it is not easy to discover the way Mark thought. Already scholars differ in their opinions on what could have been the historical circumstances and that, for a quite simple reason: we do not know who is the author of the Gospel of Mark! We do not know where he wrote his book and we do not even know precisely when he did it. Such an approach moreover instigates other problems. How can we explain that the text of Mark has had such an influence if we limit its interpretation to this historical setting? And what is the meaning of the text for today's reader if the purpose of the interpretation is limited to the historical reconstruction? Finally, whatever could have been Mark's intention in writing his story of Jesus, his text has undergone the fate of all texts. His Gospel is delivered to the interpretation created by the relationship with the reader.

What's New?

Many ask me, not without irony, "Haven't they said everything about the Gospel yet?" This question is at the same time a challenge: "Do I really have anything new to propose about Mark's Gospel?" A lot depends on the man or woman who takes this book in hand and on their presuppositions, because just like Mark's Gospel, my book is also delivered to the reader. Nonetheless, I propose the following: this book could be the beginning of a dialogue between readers. Readers of all kinds: readers familiar with Mark in their own religious tradition as well as new readers who have never read the Gospel from A to Z; modern readers sailing in the air of the time who breach philosophical questions, whether about God or the divine; readers whose engagement is rooted in the faith; readers in quest of spirituality; even readers full of critical prejudices toward the Bible and whose friends think that it is not in fashion to read a biblical book. I have written my book to be read together with the Gospel of Mark, hoping that the latter would soon occupy the central place. Its objective would be reached if readers would take the Gospel in hand and that this contact would lead them to question themselves, alone or in a group. It is not at all a question that each reader ends up with the same truth from the text. Even the story told in the Gospel is much too open for that. Since it is important that it be retranslated each time for other places and other times, uniformity is neither wished for nor realizable. The climate of the current epoch in which biblical texts function in the core of most diverse movements and religious currents and in which they even stir up from time to time a sincere interest outside this religious context, does not require a standardized reading of the Bible that would be to take or leave. To get a dialogue going on the meanings of the narrative seems to me to be an objective much more realistic for our time.

A Coded Message in Mark?

In 1901 the German biblical scholar William Wrede published a book with the title *The Messianic Secret in the Gospel of Mark.*[1] He observed that, more than the others, Mark's Gospel refused to present Jesus as the Messiah during his earthly life. The key allowing us to identify him as Messiah was only to be found after the resurrection. The most profound meaning of Jesus was not to be discovered during his life. For the whole twentieth century, seekers examined this theme in dialogue with Wrede, focusing the discussion on the question of knowing whether Jesus had been the Messiah and recognized as such before his resurrection. Let us say first of all that this

1. W. Wrede, *Das Messiasgeheimnis in den Evangelien. Zugleich ein Beitrag zum Verständnis des Markusevangeliums* (Göttingen: Vandenhoeck & Ruprecht, 1969).

historical perspective will not be our approach in the second part of this book. We will rather try to comment on the secret about Jesus from the viewpoint of the reader.

But arguments still exist to promote the idea that there is a secret in Mark. Let us risk a reading that begins with the idea that in telling his story the author foresaw two levels of meaning: on the one hand, the words that he wrote and to which everyone would have free access; on the other, a level of knowledge hidden and willingly concealed that the author would have intended only for a small elite of initiates. There are some texts in the Gospel that are susceptible to justify allusions to a code in the way that Dan Brown's famous book on *The Da Vinci Code* does. Thus, if the parables seem to have been told to all, it happens several times that Jesus takes his disciples aside to explain their meaning to them. Even this explanation, however, sometimes remains as hazy as the parable. Jesus himself mentions trusted secrets in these parables and he seems to make a distinction between one group of insiders that would seem to understand the deeper meanings and a much more numerous group of outsiders to whom these secrets would never be revealed. One of the most enigmatic texts in the Gospel says:

> Mark 4:10–12: When he was alone, those who were around him along with the twelve asked him about the parables. And he said to them, "To you has been given the secret of the kingdom of God, but for those outside, everything comes in parables; in order that 'they may indeed look, but not perceive, and may indeed listen, but not understand; so that they may not turn again and be forgiven.'"

But the text will never reveal what this mystery is precisely.

There remains still another aspect that leads to mystery. A good number of the parables and events in the story are neither explained nor clarified. Let us take as an example the expression "Kingdom of God." If scholars agree in general that this is the very essence of what Mark wants to communicate about the preaching of Jesus, it does not prevent the fact that the expression is used without anyone giving a definition. We can speak of it only through intermediary images. Other events do not receive any more explanation (I am thinking here of the miracles or again of the vision of the disciples on the mountain in which Jesus is dressed in sparkling white). Finally even the high point of Mark's story is not comprehensible either: Why did Jesus have to die on the cross, what precisely is the resurrection and what happened then to the disciples? Not a word of explanation, for example, about the resurrection. We are only told that something took place, but no one was a direct witness of it. Some women go to the tomb, but they arrive too late to "see" what had happened. There are so many parts in the Gospel that could lead a reader to suspect, even to accuse, the narrator of deliberate dissimulation. The reader could always think they are missing some indispensable, specific piece of information necessary to understand the full meaning of the Gospel. In fact, many parts of the text seem to add up to a superb detective novel on the quest of a secret code necessary to allow us to decipher the hidden message of Mark.

An Open Secret

This veil of mystery around Mark's Gospel can obviously have a certain tension as an effect. In this sense, there is a parallelism with a good number of recent novels. At the same time there exists a well-known difference on another point, a difference that comes from the negative impression that can stir up a reader of a so-called coded work. If only a few have access to the real meaning of the book, most people will have an unpleasant memory seeing that "the ultimate meaning" is denied them. They can be led to the belief that the Gospel is not true because it hides things that do not bear the light of day. This is frequently the case in our day. And the church as an institution is involved in the process because it would consciously maintain this state of things so as not to see its power and authority decline. Well then, is Mark part of these coded works? I do not think so. Obviously, the Gospel presents a mystery and we need a key to penetrate the final message of the story. But if we come to the story like detectives charged with deciphering a code, we will only be disappointed. The code that may be in question in Mark is of a completely different order than that of Dan Brown's book. The differences are significant. In Mark, there is no secret code that would lead to hidden facts outside the text. No code exists that would be intended for the happy few. No code exists that could remain under lock and key for centuries only to be revealed at a specific moment in history. The key to Mark is located in the text itself. It is at every moment within the reach of any reader. There is no concealing of information on the part of the evangelist. Each reader is able to discover the secret. At the extreme we could say that it is an open secret.

But if that is the case, why still speak of a code or a secret? The term "mystery" is indeed clearly more appropriate. Because Mark's contents are not optional and on the contrary confront readers with moments when they have to make choices and decisions. Because the book is not finished if the readers do not make the choice to open the meaning for themselves. Because ultimately, the process of reading is a process of apprenticeship. The readers unveil the secret to the extent that they answer "yes" to certain ideas in the story. Thus a successful reading of the Gospel also depends on the reader's responsibility. Obviously, there never would be a text without the initial act of an author. But from the moment that the writing is finished, responsibility for it is shared with its readers. It is even surrendered to them. It depends on the answers that they give to these options with which they are confronted that they progressively penetrate certain aspects and dimensions of Mark's message. The story is an invitation or even a challenge to make a decision and to choose. To decode the Gospel is possible only if we are conscious that the story also speaks of the reader. You have to seek in the text what are the important questions that require that we make choices. The reason Mark wrote his book in this way notably comes from the innovative—even explosive—character of its subject. The content of his description of the main character, Jesus, both as Messiah and Son of God, is not at all evident at the time in which he writes. All the same, the fact that this description insistently calls to the readers so that they take Jesus as an example to follow runs counter to the current representations of the way in which people organize their lives. The characteristic of the mystery of Mark's Gospel is very specific and is composed of two facets that cannot be separated. First of all, the reader feels gently but firmly pushed in the following sense: Jesus words and acts represent a revolutionary step in the way you should conduct yourself toward people and toward God. This is the aspect that consists of penetrating the intelligence, the recognition, and the understanding of the man that Jesus was. But the evangelist insists equally on the second aspect that refuses to separate theory from practice: he in effect wishes that we also might conduct ourselves according to the model of Jesus' own practice. The choices asked of the reader do not only have ideological conceptions concerning Jesus as their object. Even in having understood at the theoretical level, we have only partial notions of who Jesus is. Readers must also make decisions, yes or no, about the way to conduct themselves along the lines of Jesus. And my book specifically treats the way Mark has undertaken this project of integration of theory and practice at the literary level.

The idea that it is the reader who completes the meaning of the book again can usefully contribute to the current debate about the agreements between Christians and other believers. In interreligious dialogue we are sooner or later confronted with the values of our own tradition and of the principles of our faith in comparison with the whole of the many conceptions of life in general. In our focusing on Christianity, it seems that believers often use two models. For some, Christianity and its God are considered in an implicit or even explicit way as superior to the other religions or philosophies. Missionary projects often find root in this conviction. Christianity is then the universal religion that represents the only or at least the best way to redemption. In the other vision we relativize our own religion to consider it as one of the possible ways toward happiness, redemption and salvation. Christianity is then particular but equivalent to other religions. Each one of these two conceptions has difficulties: in the first, we make particularity and the value of non-Christian visions wrong; in the second, we risk not always valuing our own beliefs and traditions. It is awkward to find the exact balance that allows us to stand between these two extremes. And there will always be tensions between the two approaches. But an attractive contemporary idea could be that no philosophy or faith can prove by itself that it is right, certainly not in the expression that a universal truth would confer on them. A belief truth is born from the dialogue between sources, traditions, and a personal acceptance on the part of the "believer." Nothing in faith can be forced. It is only when belief is assumed in complete freedom at a certain moment in a person's development that deep meaning reveals itself in it. It is surprising that Mark wrote his Gospel from this perspective. Finally, it belongs to readers to decide if they find meaning in this story or not. The only thing that the evangelist does is to communicate his point of view and invite the reader to trust him.

My opinion on the Gospel is not directly inspired by these questions of interfaith dialogue. As will be established still later, the motif is rather found in the actual experience of the inaccessibility of the Bible. But a parallel exists between the two challenges of our era (interfaith dialogue and intelligibility of the Bible). A respectful dialogue between religions presupposes as a condition that people do not consider their opinions as an indisputable requirement, but as a possibility to be accomplished in their existence. A good comprehension of Mark's Gospel does not presume anything else. The text becomes understandable and takes on meaning if it is not presented to the reader as a "duty," but as a possibility, even an opportunity. That's also the approach of Mark himself. He is conscious of writing a book about questions of faith and of philosophy at the same time that he knows that we can never force people to believe. That's why he writes in a subtle way to seduce his readers so they will accept his message. Hoping that these same readers, perfectly conscious of being attracted, will agree with his story.

What Can We Expect?

This book is composed of two big divisions. Before explicitly treating the themes unique to Mark, it will be appropriate to stop and ask a few questions of a more general nature. Nowadays, the Bible is made up of "attractive unknowns." Therefore we sometimes have to take a longer view in order more to familiarize ourselves with the perspective we can have today on biblical literature. This is what the first part treats. The second will have Mark's Gospel for its object. Our starting point, consisting of reading the Gospel as a narrative, presupposes an approach that examines the specific characteristics of narrative. We call this approach "narrative criticism" or "narratological reading," while letting this term have a very broad interpretation. In such an approach to the text, it is still possible to consider three different emphases that each highlights one of the three parts of the axis of communication: the author, the text, the reader. Some emphasize the rhetorical strategy of the author (rhetorical analysis) others are interested more in the developments of plot and conflict (narrative reading in the strict sense) and still others focus on the reception of the text by the reader (reader response). I am convinced that these three approaches are complementary and cannot be separated from one another. I will continue to use the term "narrative method" to designate the whole of these ways of reading.

Obviously I have been led to make a choice among several themes that are presented in a narrative reading. We will first of all see the way the author tells stories (chapter 4) before advancing more into the content. Chapter 5, "Jesus with a Question Mark," is focused on the questions that a lot of people in the Gospel ask about Jesus, especially his opponents. In chapter 6 we will dwell upon the titles attributed to Jesus: we will in fact limit ourselves to an extensive commentary on the term "Son of God." The relations between Jesus and his disciples will be the object of chapter 7. These relations are of paramount importance for the reader, because they are mirrors: by observing how the disciples conduct themselves with Jesus, the reader in effect better understands the special character of Jesus. Finally, chapter 8 treats the passion while the epilogue contains a brief reflection on the resurrection.

For Further Reading

Bourquin, Y. *Marc, une théologie de la fragilité: Obscure clarté d'une narration.* Le monde de la Bible 55. Geneva: Labor et Fides, 2005.

Fendler, F. *Studien zum Markusevangelium: Zur Gattung, Chronologie, Messiasgeheimnistheorie und Überlieferung des zweiten Evangeliums.* Göttinger Theologische Arbeiten 49. Göttingen: Vandenhoeck & Ruprecht, 1991.

Focant, Camille. *The Gospel according to Mark: A Commentary.* Translated by Leslie Robert Keylock. Eugene, OR: Pickwick, 2012.

Telford, W. *The Theology of the Gospel of Mark.* Cambridge: Cambridge University Press, 1999.

Tuckett, C. M. "The Disciples and the Messianic Secret in Mark." In *Fair Play: Diversity and Conflicts in Early Christianity*, edited by I. Dunderberg, C. M. Tuckett and K. Syreeni, 131–50. Heikki Räisänen Festschrift; SuppNT. Leiden: Brill, 2002.

Tuckett, C. M., ed. *The Messianic Secret.* Philadelphia: Fortress, 1983. (Ten articles by different authors on the messianic secret.)

Wrede, W. *The Messianic Secret in the Gospel of Mark.* London: Lutterworth, 1987. Originally published as *Das Messiasgeheimnis in den Evangelien: Zugleich ein Betrag zum Verständnis des Markusevangeliums.* 1901. Göttingen: Vandenhoeck & Ruprecht, 1969.

2

An Antivirus Program For The Bible

A Book Eaten by Moths

VIRUSES. DO NOT TALK about them to computer users. They disturb communication or information programs and create disorder in registered data. We only need an email of an attack by a virus or an automatic worm to make a wind of panic blow over the whole planet. Without antivirus programs the software universe would not function. A short time of the breakdown of the information system in a large financial institution threatens to engender damages figuring in millions of dollars.

The Bible in its turn seems reached by viruses. Not that it expects to be attacked by one or another information pirate, far from it. The current situation of the Bible results rather from a process of long duration: the facts in the Bible are no longer or almost no longer understood and if someone believes they do understand, it does not happen very often that they can communicate these facts to people of our generation. In brief, the message of the book is no longer current. Because of good and bad use for many centuries, passages from the Bible for the most part have lost their original force or have even become squarely suspect in the eyes of a number of people. The result is a confusion and lack of interest that even widens the gap between the Bible and its readers. Let's add that the church itself, the institution in which the Book has long occupied the central place, finds itself in a state of crisis, and it is clear that the situation of the Bible is not very rosy. With a bit of realism, we need to state that not only as a founding book of a very widespread belief, but even as a more general, cultural patrimony, the Bible for many people is no more than a great unknown and therefore thus an unloved one.

Positive Signs, But . . .

Far be it from me to paint a uniformly black picture. It is indeed undeniable that in some places, such as biblical groups, certain ecclesiastical movements, or departments and centers of theology there does exist a certain interest in this very ancient book. We also observe the meritorious efforts of new social media and the possibilities offered through the internet (blogs, homepages of scholars) while it is still necessary to distrust an excessive offering in this domain and a critical attitude is needed. Without some idea about the recent developments in biblical studies, we quickly risk surfing on the waves of fundamentalist or extravagant interpretations.

Equally it happens that sometimes we meet a certain curiosity, even a desire to know more about the Bible, sometimes in private conversations. Thus, we can even state, for example, that the publication in 2004 of a new Dutch translation of the Bible stirred up the attention of the media for several weeks and therefore several hundreds of thousands of copies sold rapidly. It also was the first time that the Bible in the Netherlands had consciously been presented not only as a church book but as a literary writing having played a dominant role in Western culture. The translation committee had also been careful to present this work with the intention of reaching as large a public as possible.

But the whole question is to know if all these initiatives do not reveal precisely, in a sadder way perhaps, that the Bible currently is no more than a somewhat bizarre book and one above all incomprehensible for a large number of people. All these opportunities to read the Bible go hand in hand with a marked need for good teachings of the Scriptures. Until about 1960 the broad public hardly had need for explanations about the Bible. The environment and the places where the Bible was read were not likely to favor critical questions. I know, because I have experienced it, that the audience at conferences or biblical soirées are composed of people of a certain age who—in spite of numerous publications that very valuably inform us about the current state of things—do not always want to give a place to new ideas and continue to debate with a pile of questions. Then we too often hear remarks of the following type: "But what did they want to make us believe?" We can have very divergent opinions about the causes that have led us there. Without wanting to investigate them here, let's say that it is probably a matter of a very complex interaction between historical and cultural factors having marked the past and equally playing a role in the present. Whatever the case, we are not exaggerating when we claim that today the status of the Bible, not only that of the sacred book but also that of the cultural patrimony, is shaken and that ignorance and indifference are the principal consequences of it.

Where Do We Read the Bible? The Academic Setting

We would say therefore that there are viruses in the Bible. Isn't it time to stop a little and to disinfect? To prune the collective memory and to strip all that prevents us from seeing clearly how we can read a biblical book today? To make a *tabula rasa* in some way and begin again to construct meaning? A time of new opportunities therefore. My book represents an attempt to read a certain book of the Bible, the Gospel of Mark, in a new way, namely, by taking the questionings of the people of today as a starting point. These two parts require some clarification and I begin with the second.

I see two privileged public places—it is impossible indeed to recount what unfolds in the intimacy of a private home—where we still read the Bible in dialogue: academic settings and the church context. Let's begin with the academic universe.

In the domain of the study of the Bible, we have an overabundance of review articles and of specialized monographs. The dominant genre in the treatment of the distinct books of the Bible is called a "commentary." Most of the classical commentaries on a book of the Bible begin, in the guise of introduction, with some facts about the place, the time, and the author of the book. Then follows general circumstantial explanations for each section or subdivision of the story (called a pericope) completed by scientific commentary for each verse or word. It goes like this until the last verse of the biblical book is reached, and readers find themselves faced with a huge package of knowledge accumulated over the course of centuries that consists of different interpretations and to which the commentator compares or contrasts these with his or her own commentary and (sometimes) make a choice between them.

In itself this type of exegesis is perfectly defensible, because we cannot deny the right or the reason for existence for the *study* of the Bible. Only, in spite of the high degree of knowledge, the genre also presents some lacunas. First of all, it most of the time is intended for an academic public and above all stimulates discussion among a small number of scholars. Efforts at concretization for the general public are very rare. In addition, the explanations are often limited to questions of a philological or historical nature. We thus obtain, certainly, explanations about the Gospel in the context in which it saw the light of day, but we neglect what the meaning of the present context can bring to the interpretation. And finally, these books seem each time to be concerned essentially with the theological message intended for the target group in origin and not to produce the slightest effort to explain the pertinence of this research for today's readers. It is not by accident if the psychological approach to the Bible of Eugen Drewermann, for example, is appreciated by the general public.[1] If his method is contested by much classical exegesis because it would not correspond to the standards of *their* conception of the scholarly spirit, it is incontestable that suddenly the Bible had become readable and understandable for a large number, which has not been the case for over thirty years.

Once again, the classic scholarly works have merit. I, too, consult them regularly. But specifically at the level of the agreements between the biblical book and the present day, they sometimes leave me unsatisfied. Certainly, there are places and opportunities to discuss all these things, but there are many times when I have completely different questions concerning the Gospel. Questions that need to be laid down before the reading of a gospel (What is a gospel, for example?) that arise from life itself (What could be the relationship between Jesus' life and passion in his day and my suffering or my liabilities today?) or questions that quite simply are obstacles (Miracles do not happen, so can anything of what is written in the story be true?).

Where Do We Read the Bible? In the Church

In scholarly places with their own reviews and conferences, a neutral stance is taken to the text. This means: research unfolds without pre-established points of view, whether they are inspired by a tradition of belief or by a lack of believing tradition. But the basic question is to know whether such neutrality is possible, even desirable. Whether it is or not, I note that the separation between the two worlds is not always crystal clear. In reality,

1. E. Drewermann, *L'Evangile de Marc. Images de la rédemption*, 2 vols. (Paris: Cerf, 1993).

believers or people involved in the church participate in scholarly discourse. And there exists among scholars a multiplicity of approaches that we have to take to dialogue. Since it is a very complex question, we will later ask what is understood by "scholarly approach to the Bible." A good number of academic scholars of the Bible, in any case, refuse to be identified with the other place where the Bible is read, that is to say, the church. Because, they say, by reading the biblical story in this context, we consciously enter into a specifically believing discourse. This believing viewpoint specifies the interpretation in advance. Faith then constitutes the norm for the understanding of the Bible. There are many gradations in the methods and the realms of life for which the book has a normative value. For some, the Bible is full of ethical directives; for others, it is a book of spirituality; for yet others, it is the Word of God that contains "the unique and only Truth." Today, the number of people actively engaged in the church does not stop decreasing in the Western world. Participation in worship services diminishes. But however less numerous the groups active in church are, they remain almost always of the opinion that "the church" is the natural biotope of the Bible and that it is only there that its meaning can be fully understood.

Between Church and University

The university and the church. Although they can be contrasted, they are nevertheless the places where readers interested in the Bible find an open door. But they are at the same time places that are de facto inaccessible to most people. In affirming at the beginning of this book that my interpretation proposes to read the Gospel as a novel, I specifically hope to reach these people who, outside these academic or ecclesiastical places, care about questions of meaning and faith. It is moreover one of the remarkable phenomena of our day that the majority of seekers of meaning are outside these institutions. Some people exist who relegate the traditional church to a forgotten corner whenever there is a quest for meaning. It was not very long ago that the weekly supplement of my newspaper published about fifteen testimonies of Belgian "celebrities" on their way of seeing and living their faith, assuming as a title a quotation from one of the people interviewed: "Every intelligent person is religious." The whole thing seemed to be rather representative of the current situation. Two of these people are practicing Christians and do not want to dispense with this feeling of belonging. But the majority is no longer involved in the church's beliefs. If they have given their own content to religion, almost all of them nevertheless call themselves believers. What strikes me at the same time is the almost insignificant place of the Bible in these testimonies. And I see at the same time the almost total lack of creativity on the part of the university or the church when it comes to holding out a hand to this very large group that calls itself believing without wanting or being able to be involved with these academic or ecclesiastical places for all that. It is to this important group of seekers of meaning that I address this book. However, let one thing be clear: I am not writing to exhort people to dedicate themselves to scholarly research on the Bible. And I am not writing either to make these people come (back) into the bosom of the church. I am writing because the Gospel of Mark thrills me so much that I also want to make it resonate outside the womb of the university or the church. And it is to win this wager that I want to present the Gospel as a narrative.

Although my target group is very numerous, the text I am writing is not destined exclusively to those who are outside the university and church. On the one hand, narrative analysis that applies narrative concepts is nevertheless part of scholarly research on the Bible. The thesis that presents Mark's text as a narrative by no means signifies that it is an unjustifiable approach, without the least scholarly value. At the beginning of this book, I wanted to plead for a reading of the Bible as a novel, but that did not include the slightest judgment on my part of what is related in the Bible from a historical perspective. I only claim that the meaning of the text is revealed best when the reader allows it to be read as a narrative. Moreover, the choice of writing for a large public is not necessarily opposed to an approach in the context of ecclesiastical belief. The narrative approach to the Gospel can also reveal itself enriching for the ones who read it in the context of their faith. In brief, the Gospel can be a story for everyone. And on the other hand, if the Bible is a story for everyone, it inevitably becomes a narrative. Some thirty years ago in a small book with the very eloquent title *A Bible of Your Own*, Han Renckens wrote at the end, "The Bible is narrative. Dogmatic formulae, on the other hand, are built from carefully crafted, interlocking sets of ideas whose apparent clarity and logic can be deceptive. It is easy to forget that their origins are concrete, not abstract. They arise in long-gone mindsets and metaphors that were astoundingly fresh before they became hardened into concepts distilled from complicated, often nearly forgotten events in ages long past."[2] Progressive secularization means that still fewer people

2. H. Renckens, *A Bible of Your Own. Growing with the Scriptures*, trans. N. Forest Flier (Maryknoll, NY: Orbis, 1995) 113. Dutch original 1983.

are or want to be current with these dogmatic expressions. But forgotten dogmas do not mean the death of a narrative.

Why the Gospel of Mark?

A brief explanation to answer the question, "Why did I choose the Gospel of Mark?" will be enough. It is the earliest of the Gospels and, as much through its content as through its composition, it is the product of an author who is not so self-assured that he pretends all questions about Jesus are resolved. On the contrary, the author struggles with the questionings and tries to pierce a bit of the mystery of the public life and death of Jesus. And he confronts his readers with his own questions. Many modern readers go with him without difficulty on this journey and have the impression that this author understands them. The others, the "great" evangelists (Matthew, Luke, John) have a much clearer and surer picture of Jesus than the author of Mark. The evangelist Mark does not stop to draw attention to an important part of his thought about Jesus: that it is not at all obvious that Jesus is called "Son of God" and is recognized as such. And I think this aspect perfectly expresses what many feel today. To inquire today about the meaning of Jesus, it is good to begin with Mark. With him, we feel that knowledge of Jesus is the fruit of a relational evolution. Readers are not given objective information about Jesus, but we understand him in meeting him. Readers determine their degree of openness in view of this encounter themselves. This Gospel gives the impression of not having been written for a circle of initiates who are at the same time enlightened receivers and spreaders of certitudes. It rather refers to "all those who want to hear." If Mark's narrative is intended for everyone, that would be the basic reason for which we wish to give an interpretation that is, still today, open to everyone.

There exists another reason I have chosen the Gospel of Mark. In my opinion the heart of the book contains a revolutionary message that no one likes to hear automatically. I note it here in a single sentence because the goal of the game is that the message develops gradually as the reader penetrates more deeply into the book. To the many questions concerning the meaning of things, Mark's response is:

> Mark 10:43–44: but whoever wishes to become great among you must be your servant, and whoever wishes to be first among you must be slave of all.

If we allow ourselves to be impregnated by the idea that the main theme of the message of the evangelist is there, we understand that a lot of talent and literary creativity were necessary for the author to convince his readers to follow him and his protagonist Jesus on his way.

A New Program: Reading from the Perspective of Today's Reader

The challenge is to write about a gospel in a language that is accessible, in connection with what people are living today, without expecting them to be professional exegetes or very active in the heart of the church. This is a very conscious choice. There would be a pile of motifs to run away from before such a task. I am perfectly conscious, for example, that in scholarly circles on the Bible other criteria to take a book seriously are more prominent. Indeed it is completely possible to adopt another perspective that would have a more scholarly look: detailed research on the original context of this Gospel, for example. But I am making a choice. I am consciously deciding to seek a beginning in the present. Probably I will have to occasionally return in an indirect way to the other perspective, but in this case, I hope to be able to do it as part of a better understanding to the text today. Then in order to avoid all risk of being misunderstood, I repeat once again: So-called classical exegesis is useful, it has produced tons of information and it continues to do it. But it is not the only method, and it greatly remains inaccessible for most people.

However, there also exist positive reasons that invite us to accept the challenge that I have just mentioned. Let's realize that in the course of some thirty years, new opinions about the exact meaning of the term "scientific" have seen the light of day. The monopoly no longer belongs to the holders of the idea that the Gospel is a source of information about historical or theological facts. That is an approach that is to a large extent static. In other readings, the text functions in a dynamic way. It is instead considered as an instrument in a larger process of communication: the text makes sense because people are reading it. This explains why the text has taken on so many and different meanings all during centuries past, and why that continues, because of the people who read it and the conditions of time and place in which they read it. We probably must get accustomed a bit to the idea that the biblical text no longer has a single, exclusive meaning than any others, but that its meaning can undergo change over space and time.

In addition, the text in itself is "lazy" and expects dialogue with readers and their creativity so that a meaning can emerge. Even from the scholarly point of view, it is therefore not so stupid to look from time to time at the perspective of an actual reader to approach the text, instead of fixing on an unknown author who lived more than nineteen centuries ago.

The option mentioned summarily above is based on the differences that have taken place in hermeneutics—the study that is interested in the way we interpret and understand—in combination with what literary theories can teach us about the function of a text. Human beings see themselves more and more as assuming the role of "giver of meaning" with the result that the concept of "objectivity" is no longer as pertinent. It is rather a question of different possible perspectives that contribute to establishing meaning. Texts are not mono-semiotic and they demand to be interpreted, as patristic and medieval exegesis had moreover noted with its theory of the four meanings of the Bible. It is not possible to mention the one and only meaning of a text. But the problem of biblical texts is that they have functioned for too long in an interpretive setting that was solidly established. For many centuries the only possible interpretation has been the one that sustained the faith in the heart of the sheepfold of the church. Differences of interpretation that a text could have came from the fact that there had been several churches. Beginning with the nineteenth century, we set out on a quest for another ideal, a universal, objective interpretation according to the historical method. But that too did not seem possible any more. Sandra Schneiders justly considers it difficult to speak of the "good" or the "true" interpretation.[3] It is better to begin with the idea that there are several *valid* interpretations. And for an interpretation to be valid, it has to answer certain inevitable criteria in one or another method. The initial idea is that many methods exist to analyze a text and that each one of the methods has its own rules that lead to a better understanding of the text. To be conscious of the method we are using is to recognize at the same time that this interpretation has its limits. We concentrate on certain aspects in the text and suppress others.

A frequent reaction among the faithful is to wonder what their landmarks are if the biblical texts themselves no longer have a single meaning established once and for all. This way of reacting witnesses to tension and ambiguity. It is true that we see ourselves confronted with ourselves in our

3. S. Schneiders, *The Revelatory Text: Interpreting the New Testament as Sacred Scripture* (New York: HarperCollins, 1991) 110–27.

own tradition. With what intensity was our personal connection with the gospel? Do we only accept the gospel on the authority of others? It happens frequently that people disconnect when they state that the gospel is a much too human text. Because that pushes them to take responsibility themselves and to seek a personal meaning. It happens all too often that they not only turn their back on the church, but they also cut ties with the text. And at the same time, it is certainly a misunderstanding that is at the beginning of this reaction. Many, many people indeed think that there exists something like the only ecclesiastical interpretation of a text. This is false. Even at the heart of the community of believers, there exists sufficient liberty to use different methods in the explanation of biblical texts. In fact, a series of official commentaries of the church on the different biblical books quite simply does not exist. If we wish to inform ourselves about the most recent insights in the Roman Catholic Church concerning methodology and hermeneutics in biblical reading, we will usefully consult a document on "The Interpretation of the Bible in the Church" (1993–1994) available in English on the Internet.[4] It is true that whatever method is used in the church, it seems invariably submitted to the concern to find at least the beginning of a doctrine in the Bible. And that is precisely the stone of stumbling for a lot of people! Even in the document above, after a very good exposé about narrative method, the authors of the document could not prevent the addition that this approach must not lead to the risk of excluding all form of doctrine in the biblical texts.

If we decide to begin with the perception of readers for our book on Mark, it is because we want to propose to these readers an instrument that allows them to follow their quest for themselves. In all the realms of life, people have indeed more and more voice on the subject. Society supposes that the individual assumes more and more responsibilities. Therefore, when it concerns giving meaning, these individuals also seek their own way and are less dependent on what the institutions think instead. But they also seek guides to help them to define their opinions. This book would like to be a guide for the reading of Mark's Gospel.

4. Pontifical Biblical Commission, "The Interpretation of the Bible in the Church," April 23, 1993, http://catholic-resources.org/ChurchDocs/PBC_Interp.htm, last accessed August 2013.

The Evangelist's Intention and the Reader's Interpretation

Basically at the heart of this question, we finally find the debate over the question of knowing whether we are at the point of relating the original intention of the evangelist and -in the affirmative—if this is without more transposable to our time, beyond spatial and temporal borders. Now, in the current state of scholarly knowledge, it seems that there does not exist unanimity about the objective that the author could have had in writing his text. In other words, all exegetes currently in quest of the original intention of the evangelist inevitably put their own, so that there cannot be a question of absolute objectivity. The model of interpretation in which we considered the biblical books as bearers of historical information cannot be maintained as such. The alternative concerning the objective of exegesis is not only in the opposition between "the intention of the evangelist" and "the interpretation of the reader." The two intersect. In deciding to adopt the reader's point of view, I certainly do not deny that Mark could have specific intentions when he wrote his text. But we must admit that the evangelist and his gospel inevitably undergo the fate of any author and any text: once written, a text is delivered to the person who reads it. And all readers bring to their interpretation of a book all the established baggage of their time, of their culture, and of their personal history. So why not make of this statement a theme to be studied, giving a chance for the eventual questions of contemporary readers?

Some will insist, however, objecting: "Let's imagine for a moment the ideal state in which we would perfectly succeed in knowing the initial intentions of Mark. At that moment, the reader's role would be reduced to the minimum, wouldn't it?" From that time the question of the meaning of this ancient text would arise again for people today. How could the intentions of an author from two thousand years ago be pertinent for the present? A possible answer would be that in this case we would be at least closer to the "truth," since we would be thinking along the lines of Mark. But it is precisely there that the two coincide! Does the gospel function only in a way that allows us to transpose its established meaning to another time? And what happens if a time comes—which is perhaps already the one in which we live—in which this unique meaning has no longer any tied with the universe where people live, perhaps because they quite simply no longer understand the language and the words or that the historical and cultural circumstances have radically changed? But even against this argument, some plead for the safeguard of an original intention of the evangelist. They judge that the gospel must always prevent us from thinking in a circle and that its strength resides precisely in the fact that its message is in contradiction with the world and cannot be understood by the world. If the message is not difficult to understand or to live and is not a stone of stumbling it is no longer the gospel, they say. For them, "it is the time that is in error and the gospel that is right." This reasoning is met more frequently when Christianity lives in an era of catacombs. For this group in a minority situation, the gospel functions as an antidote against the dominant culture that is not concerned in the least about the gospel. There still, we are faced with a certain vision that comes from the idea that it is in the nature of the human being and of the culture to be opposed to what is the "good news." There is absolutely no indication that could suggest that a gospel saw the day outside Jewish, Roman and Hellenistic circles in the first century. On the contrary, early Christianity was born in this context and it bears traces of it in all its writings.

I am going rather in the sense of a thought in which the gospel and culture coexist. From time to time, the gospel is in effect in opposition, but elsewhere, it is so well in sync with life itself. This consonance independently breaks free from the seeking of the original message: it is on the contrary inferred through interpretations that locate the gospel in the time and in the culture of its reader. The gospel even has been edited so that it is comprehensible in the language, culture and mentality of the people of that day. It was sometimes in accord with the culture and its religiosity, sometimes it criticized them. In brief, the choice of our angle of attack is presently very clear. It is inspired by the consideration that, if we want to give a chance to the gospel today, it will only be possible if we give a chance to the people with their questionings today. That is the only and unique way of taking seriously the dialogue between the past and the present.

For Whom and from Whom Is the Gospel?

Let's deepen this problematic a bit. The subject is important because is tied to a cultural revolution in the frequentation of the Bible. To create an opening for a pluralism of interpretations implies in effect—as in all pluralism—that we assume our responsibility in searching meaning for ourselves while respecting the opinions of others. This does not simplify the task of the reader; on the contrary. To prefer that there is only one possible interpretation allows us to not reflect ourselves. But are we allowed, in an interpretation oriented to the reader, to accept all kinds of interpretations and make no matter whatsoever of the text? Are all interpretations valid? Not at all—we would fall then to the other extreme. We need an "ethic of reading." I borrow this expression from David Rhoads from whom I pick up some elements here.[5]

Rhoads insists on the need to grapple with the text with respect, that is to say, in the same way in which we would engage another human being. It would be absurd to try to arrive at a kind of objective approach to enter into dialogue with someone. On the contrary, we only learn to know the other to the extent that we engage and let ourselves be involved. The same is true for texts. To seek to understand texts from two thousand years ago, we need a strong dose of empathy from the readers. They need to live with and in the text in order to render the most faithful account possible. It is thus important, in the interpretation of texts, that I am conscious of factors that make my interpretation subjective—factors that make it *my* interpretation. It is up to the readers to decide with what intention they grapple with the text. One person wishes to discover the political dimension in it, another is in quest of spirituality, a third seeks a critique of the tradition, and yet another wishes to find historical foundations for their faith. To be conscious of our own starting point is important if we are reading into the gospel what we wish to read in it. In an ethic of reading, we explain our own point of view so we can better see why a text is interpreted in such and such another way. That's necessary because we thus understand not only what our critique of the text is, but also what the text questions in us. Our way to consider the role of women in Mark, for example, or to interpret the Passion of Christ, will depend on our own opinions about these subjects.

All these ideas confirm that the end product of an exegesis cannot be an objective and absolute interpretation, precisely a "finished" product. It is better to recognize that there exist "relative perspectives" that must be placed reciprocally in relationship. One of the most important components that determine the relativity of the interpretation is the fact that one belongs to one or several communities. Ethnic, social, economic, national, or religious groups in which we live determine our way of interpreting and communicating these interpretations. One of the challenges of biblical scholarship will thus be to learn to listen to the multiple differences and

5. David Rhoads, "The Ethics of Reading Mark as Narrative," in *Reading Mark: Engaging the Gospel* (Minneapolis: Fortress, 2004) 202–19.

nuances furnished by the richness of all these contexts. Dialogue with others is the only way to discover the blind points in our own interpretation. The ethic of reading is an encouragement to discover through dialogue with others where and how our own methods and interpretations need to be adjusted, refined, or nuanced. Rhoads does not hesitate to emphasize that the ethic of reading must teach us modesty.

Finally, Rhoads counsels us also about the way in which we can appropriate Mark's Gospel. It asks that readers risk questioning themselves through the text. Gospel texts have as an objective to change people. Also several questions are possible when we read Mark. Has it given us a little more hope or courage? Why? Will I be more disposed to put myself in the service of . . . ? What is this look that I have toward those who live on the margin of society? What kind of faith is important? Once again readers are in all ways free to accept these possibilities for change seriously or to reject them. But even this last attitude implies a change through the simple fact of coming in contact with the text. Rhoads cautions us against the idea that all the texts of the gospel are applicable to everyone in all circumstances. The ethics of reading imply that the reader takes account of the effect or the result of an application. Indeed, there is a big difference according to the person to whom the following saying is addressed and the circumstances in which it is used:

> Mark 9:23: All things can be done for the one who believes.

The transposition of an "old" text of authority to the present must be made with circumspection. This text will certainly have content that critiques current situations that are intolerable, but it can also contain ideas clearly out of date. Readers are responsible for their interpretation and—Rhoads says in his conclusion—these effects can only lead to life and certainly not to death.

For Further Reading

Anderson, J. C., and S. D. Moore, eds. *Mark and Method: New Approaches in Biblical Studies*. Minneapolis: Fortress, 1992 (presentation and application of several methods of reading Mark).

Best, E. *Mark: The Gospel as Story*. 2nd ed. Studies of the New Testament and Its World. Edinburgh: T. & T. Clark. 1988.

Fowler, R. *Let the Reader Understand: Reader Response Criticism and the Gospel of Mark*. Minneapolis: Fortress, 1991 (Reader response criticism and rhetorical analysis of Mark).

Pontifical Biblical Commission. "The Interpretation of the Bible in the Church (April 23, 1993; see http://catholic-resources.org/ChurchDocs/PBC_Interp.htm (page consulted on August 2013).

Renckens, H. *A Bible of Your Own: Growing with the Scriptures.* Translated by N. Forest Flier. Maryknoll, NY: Orbis, 1995.

Rhoads, D. *Reading Mark: Engaging the Gospel.* Minneapolis: Fortress, 2004 (pp. 202–19 on the ethic of reading).

Segovia, F., and M. A. Tolbert, eds. *Social Location and Biblical Interpretation in the Global Perspective.* Vol. 2 of *Reading from This Place.* Minneapolis: Fortress, 1995 (on the way the reading of the Bible is determined by its social context).

Van Iersel, B. *Reading Mark.* Translated by W. H. Bisscheroux. Edinburgh: T. & T. Clark, 1989 (Commentary on Mark from the perspective of the reader).

Van Oyen, G. "Changing Hermeneutics in Reading and Understanding the Bible: The Case of the Gospel of Mark." In *Hermeneutics, Scriptural Politics and Human Rights: Between Text and Context*, edited by Gaay Fortman, B. de, K. Martens, and M. A. M. Salih, 99–121. New York: Palgrave Macmillan, 2010.

3

Before Reading: Eliminate the Misunderstandings

Introduction

This chapter is intended for readers who do not spontaneously choose a book on the Bible for their personal libraries. As an author, this obviously poses me a problem, for the whole question is to know if a chance exists that they will ever pick up this little book, and if they do if they will before long close it and put it aside and thus never reach this chapter. In this case, I comfort myself by saying to myself that several of the ideas that follow may also interest an already convinced public and that in it there very well might be some people who will speak of it to those around them.

In the preceding chapter we stressed the difficulties that come from the nature of the Bible itself. Let's now look at the barriers that risk arising from the side of the readers. That the books of the Bible no longer count among the best-sellers comes not only from the gulf that separates the era of the origins of the Book from our contemporary world. In the secularized West, a dominant critical attitude to the Bible undeniably runs between indifference, ignorance, and aversion. If I limit myself to the West, it is because, all during a two-year stay in the Congo, I had the experience that it is especially in the West that the Bible is an ignored or criticized book. Once we cross the borders of a Western European or a Northern American hyper-materialist world—with a slight apology for this somewhat wide-ranging characterization and generalization—we meet cultures that resort to the Christian source texts in one way or another or to other religious traditions. There they know the Bible without criticizing it. This statement does not imply the slightest reproach to either position. The uncritical approach to the Bible in parts of the non-Western world has given birth to its own problems, but that is not the subject that occupies us here. The fact is that history developed differently in the West; the course of events could have perhaps been slowed down, but it could not be stopped. That's why this thesis is irreversible: if we find that it is important that today people read the Bible, we have to keep in mind the fact that we no longer live in a universe oriented by and to the Bible. We thus have to respect the culture and the mindset that dominates here and now. The word "respect" may seem a bit odd in this context, but I am convinced that if we do not bear in mind what lives in the target group, every word about the Bible risks being counterproductive. If we are not open to what exists in today's society, every effort of beginning an intelligent conversation about the Bible in a larger circle is bound to fail. The first step toward good communication can be to correctly state a few misunderstandings that are very widely spread concerning the Bible.

We have admitted for a long time already that we no longer have to look for the main causes of the negative reaction to the Bible in the individual responsibility of each modern person. It results far more from an ancient history that is now several centuries old that has led to a series of misunderstandings and misinterpretations about the Bible. It is these misinterpretations—moreover often transformed into prejudices that may be thoughtless or not, it is true—that make it impossible again to pick up precisely this book. From a practical point of view, the Bible has disappeared from current life to such an extent that we no longer understand any longer the book in question. It remains for many people a hermetical book. This chapter hopes to try to draw up a short inventory that prevents people consciously or unconsciously to even try to open the Bible or begin a reading on the Bible. It is the unique pretension of these pages, because to attack in a few pages cleaning out all the misunderstandings that have developed over centuries would be an impossible mission. Most of the time they are deeply anchored in people's intuition. Since to fight misunderstandings so present in the collective consciousness equals the work of Sisyphus, I will limit myself to exposing three of them.

The Bible Is Not "True"

The biggest misunderstanding about the Bible is probably the one associated with the words "true" and "truth." In our current language and feeling we have conferred on the word "truth" a main nuance of historical exactness. It is a deeply rooted opinion that closely follows the opinions of the thinkers of the century of Enlightenment. The misunderstanding comes from the temptation to consider every literary source as a source of information intended to accurately convey historical facts. Further, if we consider that only historically accurate information has the right to call itself "true," we display a specific vision of the truth that unfortunately applies to a very restricted number of documents. It is an idea very broadly expanded that, to be reliable, the Bible must be historically true. Often, people no longer turn to biblical texts because they have "discovered" that the Bible seems to contain "errors." Which means in their eyes that the biblical events could not have taken place as they are written. It is one way of seeing that is the result of specific ideas concerning the notion of "truth." Ever since then, under the guise of counter-reaction, it is usual to ask the question if all texts have been written with the intent to inform readers about historic dates. And, to address our subject without further delay, "Was the Bible written as a historical book, by and for historians?" To ask the question is to give the answer: the way the Bible originated does not require us to consider it as a book of history. We do not have the opportunity to deepen this question here, but every good introduction to the Bible is dedicated to treat this theme in extenso. I am content to send you to the first three chapters of the book of the Belgian exegete Peter Schmidt on historicity and truth in the Gospels. The author there explains how the symbolic presence of God in Jesus is realized through the texts.[1]

Furthermore, the concept "scientific," according to which historical authenticity asserts itself as the indisputable criterion by which to judge the truth of something, presents a problem. From the precise scientific viewpoint, we have long ago arrived at the conclusion that a piece of information is only very rarely "purely" historical. Neutral information does not exist. We could probably consider exceptions such as the communication of concrete data concerning place and time, but even these data are often susceptible to interpretation. All sources, whether texts or archaeological

1. P. Schmidt, *How to Read the Gospels: Historicity and Truth in the Gospels and Acts*, trans. C. Vanhove-Romanik (London: St. Paul, 1993).

elements, still contain a piece of interpreted information that, in addition, demand interpretation to become significant. In other words, data in themselves do not have meaning. They get it only when they are "understood" by someone. Data in themselves tell us nothing. As they are always surrounded by interpretation, it is necessary to examine every time and individually to the extent the datum is trustworthy at the historical level. This research can moreover very well lead to the conclusion that the text in question was not intended in the least to transmit an exact piece of information. The big misunderstanding then consists of denying all meaning to this text. The reverse is true: it is because they contain interpretation that texts have meaning. And since we interpret them in turn, they obtain a new meaning.

Then is the Bible true? What is valid for all historical sources is true also for the Bible. To know if the Bible contains historical data, we need to examine it according to the established rules of historical criticism. Nothing new so far—that has been done for several centuries. Moreover the results are interesting. First of all, it is not possible to advance in a general way that the Bible is historically true or false. It is appropriate to examine separately every word and event and to question its eventual link with history. Second, a large variety of literary genres exist. Only a small number of biblical texts were written with the intent to furnish historical information. Very often texts seek to express an interpreted reality, notably, the way in which God is experienced in the world, the cosmos, history, and people. To seek a historicity in which there are not any interpreted realities in any way would inevitably lead to misunderstandings. We do not expect a myth to be historically accurate. The first chapters of Genesis do not contain historical truth, and even if they intend to relate the history of origins, they obviously answer in no way to our criteria about the historicity of the events reported. We can verify if a parable could have been told by Jesus or not, but not if the narration of the parable really took place. Proverbs express by general statements or by concrete examples what people have acquired through experience and that they wish to pass on as good counsel. The Psalms are prayers.

But there is a third point. Whereas the majority of researchers have followed the developments of critical exegesis, some—among whom are scientists—try by all means to defend and prove the historical truth of the Bible. They are only a minority, it is true, but since they defend such an obvious thesis, they exercise an often unconscious great influence. Their conviction that the Bible is historically exact is determined by their faith and tradition. Reading a book or commentary about the Bible, it is important to be informed to know where the wind blows. And, unless one is personally convinced that all that the Bible contains is historically exact, in general one very quickly senses whether the faith of the researcher determines for him the historical veracity of the Bible. Reasoning generally goes this way: "Since the Book is the Word of God, I believe it and it must be historically true." The faith of these people is auxiliary to the trustworthiness of the Bible. If the latter is shaken, the whole of their edifice of faith crumbles. This form of conviction cannot be useful either to faith or historical science. Thus, people rejecting the Bible because it is not historically true, in addition to those who swear by it as an historical book, in fact base their conviction on the same misunderstanding.

The only reply to this misunderstanding is that the Bible does not *need* to be historically true. There does not exist a single reason for which the biblical text has decisively to render an account of a historical reality. The intention of the biblical authors, even when they intend to tell history, and the truest history possible, that is, history as God sees it, is not to encourage the examination of the accuracy of the historical information. And the first hearers of the biblical narratives did not turn to the Bible either to verify the exactitude of facts according to the historiography of the time. Ever since, why would current readers fix themselves only on the historical aspect of the Bible? If at the end of research it seems that a specific passage in the Bible is really historical, it is certainly an interesting discovery, but that does not confirm or reject in any way the credibility of the Bible. All this leads us to a necessary clarification of concepts concerning truth. Historical truth cannot be a category according to which we could judge whether the Bible is a book that merits reading or not. In scientific-critical circles this idea has made its way for a long time. When people allude to the "truth" in speaking of the Bible from their religious conviction, they mean something else. To acknowledge a text or a person can only be the result of a long process of association with this text or this person. We discover, for example, that the content of this text is worth the trouble only insofar as it is a source of inspiration for our lives. From then on, the text is not judged according to the criteria of historicity, but according to the following question: "Does its content—but there we have to appeal to metaphors—give life, create space, prove fruitful?" In this sense, the truth of the Bible is itself a metaphor: it is a picture we can use to express that the story of the Bible obtains for us a perspective full of meaning for our lives.

To Read the Bible You Have to Be a Believer in the Church

A lot of people never pick up a Bible because they think that it is a book for believers. They do not wish to identify with a believer because of his churchly side. In our time, the image of the church is certainly not likely to draw crowds. No one will deny that the Bible has really proved itself in the religious tradition of the church and that it has guided that religious tradition. But there is a difference between recognition of the Bible, on the one hand, and the opinion that you have to be a believer and belong to a church to read the Bible, on the other. Perhaps we could say: the church has been the place in which we have traditionally read the Bible as believers. And most of the readers of the Bible perceive themselves in one way or another connected to a church.

But in our time, a problem raises itself: What does being a believer mean? An inquiry about faith in a sufficiently large group of people probably would lead to remarkable statements, quite like that of the diversity in the ways of living our faith at the heart of any group that calls itself believing. It has appeared thus in an investigation that an important number of those who call themselves Christian do not believe in the resurrection but rather in reincarnation, whereas the resurrection—as opposed to reincarnation—is a fundamental tenet of the Christian faith. We state equally, still in the heart of the believing community, how ideas about the Bible, prayer, politics, the image of God, revelation, or interreligious dialogue can be different. The fundamentals of the faith can be interpreted in very different ways. In addition, we discover that a lot of those who call themselves non-believers nevertheless have admiration for the person of Jesus and are interested in what he was. Many non-believers do not distinguish themselves in any way from Christians when social justice, solidarity, respect for the rights of human beings, or respect for the religion of others is concerned. Some call themselves religious without however wanting to join traditional institutions. The sketch of the border between believers and non-believers is no longer parallel to the one that separates those who are in the church and those who prefer to remain outside.

This is why I plead for a new dialogue about meaning and spirituality beyond the borders of the institution of the church. And one of the ways to build a bridge is the Bible. This will probably require considerable effort from both sides, especially efforts to listen. It will not be necessary for those who are in the church to try to prove by all means that they are right for the single motif that in their tradition they know very well how they have to understand the Bible. The idea of an objective interpretation of the Bible is indeed passé. And those who live outside the church probably will not find it obvious to read a book that has always been identified with the tradition of this church. But perhaps the postmodern era creates favorable conditions to germinate this kind of dialogue. The seekers for meaning are all very receptive to words of wisdom that have been transmitted for centuries. I will come back several times to the theme of faith in the course of this book.

The True Meaning Is Hidden

I said earlier in connection with the *Da Vinci Code* that books on the so-called hidden dimensions of religion are actually a hit. This is a remarkable and paradoxical phenomenon, because readers who for a very long time have not been at all informed about the state of biblical things instantly acknowledge what seems sensational and goes against "traditional" beliefs. The explanation is probably found in what has already been stated earlier: they do not feel themselves at home in the usual setting where the Bible is read. This is why they create their own "new" gospels or discover old apocryphal (which means "hidden") gospels upon which to found a new belief. This process is nourished moreover by the conviction that if these texts have remained hidden for a long time, there must have been a plot fomented in the heart of the ecclesiastical hierarchy in place.

As to what concerns the new tendency of beliefs, it is not that people feel the need to adopt a critical attitude. The uncritical attitude toward newly discovered texts is inversely proportional to the critical attitude toward classic biblical texts. We recognize moreover a recurring model. A book is published on the theme of hidden verities. It can be about the Scrolls discovered near the Dead Sea that reveal that Jesus was not the founder of a new religion or the gnostic writings from Nag Hammadi that reveal revolutionary ideas about Christianity. When I wrote this book, journals were overflowing with articles dedicated to the announced publication of the Gospel of Judas. And once again, this "hidden text" must produce a picture of Jesus different from that of the four canonical Gospels. And once more, the public swallowed it without the slightest critical reflection. A strange phenomenon that everyone so easily turned to hypotheses or broken-down reconstructions without foundation. For in what concerns apocryphal texts, we can indeed settle for a lot less certainty about history, context, place, and date of origin than for texts that are represented in the biblical canon. Nevertheless these so-called revolutionary theories are acknowledged without a problem as an alternative to the biblical tradition.

We know plenty of elements and causes that explain this phenomenon, but we will not here go into depth about possible theological, sociological, or psychological motifs. I stop only for a moment on an element that concerns the texts themselves. There exists a misunderstanding about the value of "hidden" texts and their relation with texts that have been known for a long time such as the Bible. Spontaneously, we could have the impression that texts that have lasted a long time in the shadows are more trustworthy than known classical texts. We suspect the latter to contain "false truths" to which people would have wrongly adhered for centuries. In this debate, I would like to plead in favor of more realism and lucidity. The discovery, publishing, and diffusion of apocryphal texts in fact give no reason to not read the Bible. On the contrary, we better understand apocryphal texts by placing them side by side with the Bible. And the reverse is equally true. The reading and study of non-canonical texts makes us better understand the Bible. Thus, it is undeniable that there were in the whole of the early church tensions and different ideas concerning the New Testament and the apocryphal texts about Jesus. Even the New Testament is moreover a synthesis of different approaches to the person of Jesus. Apocryphal texts are interesting because they reveal what litigious points could have played a role during the first centuries. They emphasize specific points or favor certain aspects of the ancient traditions. In other words, if we want to have a more precise and complete look at the developments of early Christianity, knowledge of writings "unknown" until now is indispensable.

This pragmatic approach can help us temper emotional reactions that invite overvaluation of apocryphal texts. The fact that they have remained hidden does not alone make them more original or trustworthy than the canonical texts. It is only by comparing all texts (apocryphal and canonical) that we will have any idea of the pictures of Jesus and God that circulated in the time of early Christianity. It is from there that it is possible for readers to better choose which tradition they prefer. In addition, it is really too stupid to radically contrast canonical and apocryphal texts. They have in truth many things in common and they are ultimately rooted in the same tradition. From a historical point of view, it is clear that at the end of several centuries, a consensus was formed in the heart of the church about a series of texts that they wanted to collect and consider as foundational texts. As other apocryphal texts appear, they can invite us to interesting discussions about the meaning of Jesus. At each discovery of a new writing, we can relive now a bit of what could have happened many centuries ago. We go back in time and we discover each time a new element that contributes to the discussion about the person of Jesus. We will see moreover that today's discussions do not differ very much from disputes of other times. But there is not the slightest advantage to say that either the apocryphal or the canonical texts are taboo. Much to the contrary, if sincere "seekers for meaning" want to deepen their knowledge of Christianity, they can only gain by collecting as many sources as possible. It is only from these sources that they will be able to make a personal choice. The backwaters that provoke the spread of "unknown" texts constitute a positive argument for starting a (re)reading of the "known" texts.

Conclusion

At the end of this first part, I want to express a wish: that on behalf of the individual, the church, and the whole society, the Bible can become an open book that can be discussed in the public square. I think that must progressively be possible in our days. Bearing in mind the extent of secularization, we begin by taking, whether inside or outside the church, a different look on the strength that has been that of the church. The threatening side of the institution has declined strongly. There are elements that allow religion to (re)gain a place in the personal agenda and that of society. For, humans always find their way back to religion. The crisis of traditional forms of celebration is not the death of religion. It would be a missed opportunity if the Bible did not have a voice in this chapter of religion's development. On the personal level, people are certainly much freer than before to pick up a Bible and obtain a contribution to their own vision about life and the world. This will show itself without any doubt on a much more colorful palette than ever before. Likewise in debates of civilization about multicultural society or ethical questions, it is important that a lot of people—believers and non-believers—have a correct picture of what the Bible is. It is a sine qua non condition of reciprocal respect and a guarantee that there will not be a bad use of the Bible. I have therefore wanted to show in this first part that even the Bible is an open book, accessible to everyone. In the second part, we will try to apply these ideas to the Gospel of Mark. Every reader can go with us in the quest for challenges with which this evangelist confronts us.

For those who would like first to read the text of the Gospel, the presentation of the structure below is probably useful. It can also serve to correctly place the references or the quotations that we will be led to mention in the whole of the Gospel.

Structure of Mark's Gospel

Several structural proposals for the Gospel of Mark have been made. That which follows is not based on geographical facts, but it tries to take account of several important themes in the Gospel: the relation between Jesus and the disciples, the lack of understanding of the disciples, the opposition to Jesus, the Passion. It is always difficult to know whether the author truly intended to structure his Gospel in such and such a manner. The most important thing about a structure is that it is "useful." By a continual coming and going between the structure (which is static) and the plot (which is much more dynamic) the reader tries to find the confirmation of a few central themes of the text. We have consciously opted for the narrative of the empty tomb (Mark 16:1–8) as the ending of the Gospel. Most exegetes see in this narrative the original ending of Mark. Verses 9 to 20 that are found in the majority of modern translations because they have been accepted as "canonical" in the ecclesiastic tradition have been added later to the tradition. They were written by a scribe who knew about the resurrection appearances and the sending of the disciples that we find in the other Gospels. In addition, as we will see in the last chapter of this book, the "short" ending that occurs in Mark 16:1–8 is more in agreement with the general interpretation of the Gospel: it is the reader who has to respond to the challenge of the message of the young man dressed in white going about to search for the resurrected Christ.

1:1 The theme of the book: good news, Jesus Christ, Son of God

1:2–13 Prologue: readers are informed about the background and the identity of Jesus

1:14—8:26

First Part: The attraction that the a-bit-strange person of Jesus has fulfilled, especially in Galilee, arouses all kinds of reactions in the entourage of Jesus, as

	much in his disciples as among religious authorities. This invites the readers to reflect on the identity of Jesus.
Transition *a*	1:14–15, 16–20 Synthesis of the message about the Kingdom of God and call of the first disciples.
1:21—3:6	**Jesus brings his liberating message to his homeland. First conflicts.**
1:21–45	First meeting with Jesus as an exorcist and healer.
2:1—3:5	The behavior of Jesus involves a conflict with the authorities.
3:6	Negative remark: the authorities think explicitly about doing away with Jesus.
Transition *b*	3:7–12, 13–19 Jesus attracts the crowds; installation of the twelve disciples.
3:20—6:6	**The words and acts of Jesus become stronger and stronger. He wins success but also arouses resistance and lack of understanding.**
3:20–35	Criticism of the opponents and family
4:1–34	Parables and comparisons on the Kingdom of God.
4:35—5:43	Jesus' authority is shown in miracles.
6:1–6a	Negative remark: resistance and lack of understanding in his birthplace.
Transition *c*	6:6b-7–13 The mission of the disciples in view of the extension of Jesus' activities.
6:14—8:26	**More numerous and powerful miracles but increasing lack of understanding among the disciples.**

6:14–29	Flashback: the death of John the Baptist
6:30–56	Miracles near the lake
7:1–23	New conflicts: discussion about purity
7:24—8:10	Other miracles, this time also outside the borders of Galilee
8:11–21, 22–26	Negative remark: the disciples' lack of understanding (11–21) followed by the healing of a blind person in two steps (22–26).
8:27–30	**Hinge moment for the disciples and the readers: "Who am I according to you?"**
8:31—10:52	
Second Part:	In his own company, resistance to Jesus who announces his passion. The disciples' attitude as a mirror for readers. On his way to Jerusalem Jesus teaches about the characteristics of the Kingdom of God and the conditions to reach it. This section is expanded around the triple announcement of the passion:
8:31, 32–33, 34–9:1	Announcement of the passion followed by the lack of understanding of the disciples and by the teaching of Jesus.
9:31, 32, 33–37	Announcement of the passion followed by the lack of understanding of the disciples and by the teaching of Jesus.
10:32–34, 35–40, 41–45	Announcement of the passion followed by the lack of understanding of the disciples and by the teaching of Jesus.
11:1—15:47	

Third Part:	The death of Jesus. The behavior of his opponents and his disciples incites the readers to choose: Is it possible for them to believe in a crucified Messiah? Near Jerusalem and in the city.
11:1—13:37	The teaching of Jesus in the temple. Opposition of the authorities. Future perspective for the temple, the universe and the message of Jesus.
11:1–25	The entry of Jesus into Jerusalem and his vision on the temple.
11:27—12:44	Confrontation with the religious leaders over power.
13:1–37	Transition from the present time to the new time.
14:1—15:47	Jesus is abandoned by everyone, he is condemned and dies on the cross. The reader remains alone first with an agonizing Jesus and then with a dead Jesus.
14:1–42	Jesus and his disciples are together for the last time.
14:43—15:15	Arrest and condemnation.
15:16–47	Crucifixion, death and placing in the tomb

16:1–8

Open ending: Traces of a new beginning

SECOND PART
Mark's Gospel

4

How Does the Evangelist Narrate?

Introduction

"ALL RIGHT, HAVE YOU read the last Harry Potter? What is it about? Can you tell me the story?" We admit in general that in reading, most people seek to know the contents: What happens, what's it about? Indeed, it could go the same way for the Gospel. However, it is not a concern at present to recount what is in the Gospel or to make a synthesis of the content. We indeed have the feeling that everything is on the same level of importance and that we would have to take up each of the episodes one after the other. A synthesis could not, for example, allow us to omit Jesus' baptism or the fact that he forgave sins or that he fed five thousand people or again that he predicted the destruction of the temple or . . . As the gospel story is composed of a series of anecdotes, it gives the impression of not having a continuous narrative line. And things become even more complex when we begin to ask theological questions as, for example, why Jesus is the Son of God. Perhaps many people would answer that, in Mark, it is not so obvious that Jesus is the Son of God. We could expect a bit more clarity and explicit language on the part of the evangelist. It is not really surprising that Mark has been considered for many centuries a poor writer.

Is that really the case? Has our first evangelist not succeeded in sharing with his public a passionate story? Or is this negative judgment essentially the act of exegetes having always neglected to consider the text of Mark as a narrative? Scholars have often divided the narration into numerous small passages so that it became difficult to have an experience of reading the whole book. Moreover, they focused on the historical context of each episode. By making a play on words we could say, "Too much history, not enough story." Nevertheless, to inquire about the way the author communicates with his readers presupposes that we consider the Gospel in its whole as a narrative. An atomization or a division into short passages turns our attention away from the process of reading to questions about details in the separate parts. Happily, the ideas of certain literary theories in the secular sector have gained ground in the study of the Bible. And we must say that over the course of the last three decades attention has generally come to the Gospel of Mark.

From a methodological viewpoint, we mention a slide from a diachronic method of reading toward a synchronic method. The first emphasizes the "strata" of which the text is composed in order to draw near to the historical core as close as possible. It is as if we were clearing away the text by successive slices (*dia*-chronic). In the second, we consider the narrative elaboration of a text by interpreting the events as part of the text as it is presented (*syn*-chronic). An important part of these new methods is that they give us the right to say anything about the text only after an exhaustive reading. That's why we will dedicate the following chapters to the narrative line concerning Jesus (chaps. 5 and 6) and the disciples (chap. 7). But it is another aspect of this narrative reading that I wish to treat before beginning the "what" of the text. It concerns the language and style of the text. In literary analysis, it is the part of the study that we call "rhetorical" or the "how" of the writing of the text. It is then no longer so much a question of the plot (What happened, when, where, and with whom?) but of the way in which the evangelist has fashioned the events narrated.

The commentary on the way the author communicates implicitly or explicitly with his readers by using certain rhetorical elements or by introducing stylistic characteristics is an open door to whomever. It is a form of literary criticism. The objective of this commentary is to prove that the evangelist is a good narrator and that he does everything in his power to direct his readers' attention to the narration. Concerned to direct to a large diversified public, I deem this analysis to be the most needed because it broaches the text at the literary level. There is very little need, if any at all, for either preliminary scholarly knowledge or faith in the gospel. The analysis does not have as an objective to convince people of the truth of a text, but to open their eyes to the qualities of the narrator. It reveals passionate aspects of the text that permit every individual to better see that the text possesses in itself the force to influence readers. But at this stage, it is absolutely not required that they agree or disagree with the contents of the gospel. In the end, the readers will have to determine whether they want to go deeper in their study of the text and how.

The "How" of a Narrative

Authors hoping to convince readers will use certain literary elements, rhetorical or narratological, in their style to capture and keep their readers' attention and finally to lead them to have an opinion. In the best of cases, these readers will assume the narrator's vision. Good narrators know that they have to build up tension and trigger with the readers emotions or feelings of approval, doubt or sympathy. It is even more necessary that the readers feel themselves challenged by the text if this text is meant to convince people of certain ideas or even to influence their attitude or their behavior. In brief, if authors expect to succeed in spreading their message, it will be necessary to win over the public's favor. Recent ideas about the narrative character of the Gospels have demonstrated that *the way* in which a Gospel has been constructed determines the *content* given in the narrative as well. In other words, form and content are a pair. This is an important fact. In fact, many of these literary conceptions are rooted in the art and the rules of ancient rhetoric. But for long centuries, the gospel texts have been carefully armored against all rhetorical analysis. Perhaps because we have conferred on them a too sacred character and/or we wished not to open them up to the literary—and therefore human—view of their origins. But things have changed and before concretely considering the content of the Gospel, I propose to examine the literary form that Mark has given to his Gospel with the goal of influencing the process of reading.

The Anonymous Narrator

Scholars have invested a lot of energy in their desire to identify the author of the Gospel according to Mark. Moreover, for each of the books of the Bible this question of authorship has largely maintained the attention for many centuries, the underlying idea being that if we could identify the "home port" and the identity of the author, we could reach a correct evaluation of the trustworthiness of the text. In this sense, it was important for the interpretation of the Gospels that we could place the evangelists as close as possible to Jesus. As scholars agreed in concluding that Mark could not have known Jesus, they sought a connection through the means of Peter. An important figure and an eyewitness, Peter would thus be the "missing link," allowing us to guarantee the credibility of the Gospel. Still today there remain scholars who follow this path and for whom the message of this Gospel passes or breaks on the basis of their vision of the status of the author Mark as an historical person. They are, however, only a minority.

Narrative exegesis reverses things. It begins with the idea, shared today by the majority of scholars, that the author of the gospel is an anonymous Christian who wrote this text around the year 70 of the first century CE. And if he had wanted to make historical accuracy a theme of his writings, he would undoubtedly have treated it in a more explicit way. He has not done this. Does that weaken the credibility of his book? On the contrary, in disappearing into anonymity, he specifically acquires authority since, in this way, the message is no longer dependent on the specific vision of an individual author located in such-and-such a year in such-and-such a place. As an author he relies on the stage-effects. He does not write in the first person, thus the narrative itself occupies the forefront of the scene. Our whole attention can be concentrated on the events concerning the principal character, Jesus.

The Reliable "Omniscient" Narrator

The establishment of a relation between the narrator and reader is absolutely indispensable, so that the reader is put on the right road that the narrator is presented as a person worthy of trust. If ever the readers risk having doubts about the serious character of the narrator, there is little chance they will take his message seriously. Here, without the narrator unveiling his identity, he succeeds in passing for an author invested with authority. In order to do this, the fact of creating himself as an omniscient narrator has been of a determining weight. Thus he directs the setting of his story. At the simplest level, we can already say that what is proposed to the readers as a collection of facts is in reality a composition cleverly elaborated by the narrator. He puts on the stage people that he causes to come in contact with Jesus. By comparing the narrator to a cameraman, we see that he takes the liberty of moving his camera from one place to another. He gives close ups and from time to time a panoramic view. He it is, too, who succeeds in directly creating a tension by arousing situations of conflict between Jesus and the holders of power. He is the one who decides to make the disciples fluctuate between trust in Jesus and lack of understanding of him. He it is who decides to begin with the baptism of Jesus and end with the empty tomb. He does not in the slightest way mention the history concerning Jesus' birth, no more than there are appearances of Jesus after the resurrection.

Readers scarcely stop to think of the fact that all this is interpretation. The narrative passes as authentic and believable. As readers travel in thought, so to speak, in the omniscience of the narrator, the feeling comes to them of mastering the narrative themselves and thus to accept that what is told is true. No one knows as much about all these events as the author and . . . the readers.

The author's omniscience is particularly evident when he is reading and expressing the interior thoughts of people. Thus it is that he tells that the Pharisees plot among themselves to get rid of Jesus. He is equally present when some disciples discuss among themselves about their place in the Kingdom of God. He again knows perfectly when Jesus brings to light the thoughts of people he meets: he detects their faith, their hostility, their questioning, and their feelings. This last part, that Jesus possesses a great deal of intelligence about the people around him is important. It creates the idea that the narrator and Jesus think in the very same way. The narrator evolves, so to speak, in parallel with the thoughts and acts of Jesus. In the eyes of the reader, the narrator shares the quasi-totality of the norms and ideas of Jesus. The narrator and Jesus constitute a unanimous duo.

Omniscience Again: Space . . .

From the beginning of the twentieth century, the idea among exegetes increases that the geographical data and the chronological evolution in Mark are created by the author himself. Recent studies confirm it and try equally to discover the deeper significance of these structures. There is therefore a geographical division contrasting two large blocks, Galilee and Jerusalem, that is not simply a geographical fact. It is also a contrast between two conceptions of the religious life. Through this geographical contrast, the narrator confronts his reader with two fundamentally different approaches to the religious life. It is not by chance that Galilee is exactly the location where the good news, the gospel, is proclaimed. The narrative stresses in several places the fact that Jesus came from Galilee, which is also the place where he works. And the last words of the young man in the white robe in the empty tomb encourage the women to return to Galilee to meet the resurrected Lord there. Galilee symbolically represents a religion accessible to the common person. Jerusalem is the region that shows itself hostile to Jesus. The city of Jerusalem is not only the symbol of the religious center; it is also the place where the heart of official Judaism actually rules. It is this city in which the political and religious hierarchies share the power that becomes the strongest opposition to Jesus. It is there that the end of Jesus' life occurs. At each step that Jesus takes toward Jerusalem, the tension of a very serious threat raises a notch. The reader is irresistibly affected by it. Jesus keeps to his own way of coming into God's presence, which is different from the official practices current at the time.

There's another aspect of this spatial perspective that should guide the reader. If the narrative clearly makes a distinction between two levels in the cosmic world, it does not hesitate to constantly bring them together. They are, on the one hand, the earthly level in which the story telling of the interpersonal tensions between human beings and, on the other, the heavenly realm in which a similar tension between the higher powers occurs. Mark shares this idea of earthly and heavenly spheres with his contemporaries; it is certainly not an idea that is his own. In a religious apocalyptic perspective, nothing happens on the earth that is not a reflection of the transcendent heavenly spheres, the natural habitat of demons, angels, and God. Thus, the conflicts on earth between Jesus and the authorities, for example, have their antipode in the conflicts between the demons and God in the heavenly universe. Likewise, God can very well send a messenger—an angel—if he wants to make a signal or send a message to human beings. This appears obviously a bit strange to the current reader who conceives of the immensity of the universe with a scientific cosmology. It is, by way of contrast, a perfectly normal fact in a view of the world based on an ancient religious cosmology. We are confronted by a characteristic example of the gulf that separates their world from ours, such as we pointed out in the first chapter. The reader has to take into account that we do not live any longer in this mental world. To end up giving meaning to this phenomenon, we have to seek another level than that of a literal interpretation of a kind of physical interference between these two spheres. To seize precisely this interpretation in modern terms is not easy, but the orientation of the evangelist's message is certainly clear: what comes through the coming of Jesus has a profound significance that overturns the current opinions about God and his connections to the world. Jesus' attitude is determinative for the way we think of the transcendent. If it is possible to read history at the strictly human level, the narrator indicates to the reader in every way that it would be a narrowing of Jesus' perspective. We will come back to this later, but it is already evident that we are touching here on the essential part of the picture that the narrator forms of Jesus. This perspective on Jesus is multiple or at least double: an earthly vision of Jesus is possible but, in the eyes of the narrator, it is incomplete and has to be enriched by a perspective from the transcendent universe. Human beings have, just like God, a look at Jesus.

. . . and Time

We can have the impression that Mark has imposed limits with regard to the lapse of time covered by his narrative that in the end includes only a few fragments of a few months of Jesus' life. But this, too, proves his art of orienting the interpretation of the history. By placing the earthly aspect of Jesus' existence in a temporally enlarged context, the reader receives as evidence the impression that the meaning of Jesus' action is universal and atemporal. Through the coming of Jesus the past as well as the present and the future have changed. This process takes form, moreover, from the beginning of the Gospel. The narrator indeed implies the story of the history of Israel in the explanation of the meaning of Jesus.

> Mark 1:2–3: As it is written in the prophet Isaiah, "See, I am sending my messenger ahead of you, who will prepare your way; the voice of one crying out in the wilderness: Prepare the way of the Lord, make his paths straight."

The fact that the Gospel begins with a quotation—in fact, a mixture of several texts from the Old Testament—shows that Jesus did not suddenly fall from the sky without warning, but he fulfills an expectation. Through Jesus comes the demonstration that the prophets were right (1:2–3). Jesus is the answer to the current hopes of Israel. The past makes sense because it is from now on possible to interpret it in a pertinent way. It is therefore difficult to overestimate the importance of the quotation. It occurs not only right at the beginning of the Gospel, but it is in addition the only time that the *narrator* quotes Scripture to explain the narrative. The good twenty-something other times in which important quotations from Scripture will always be in discussions between Jesus and his disciples or his opponents.

On the other hand again, Jesus finds himself placed directly in the story. He is characterized in the most concrete sense of his humanity. It is in this place and this moment in history that he has his place:

> Mark 1:9: In those days Jesus came from Nazareth of Galilee and was baptized by John in the Jordan.

Impossible to be more concrete. We will notice that the first word that Jesus pronounces also concerns time: "The time is fulfilled . . ." (1:14b). That's an expression that alludes to its own action, but at the same time each present moment. The significance of these words is not so much that the chronological unfolding (the *chronos*) stops for a moment to announce a specific intervention and then time takes up its course again. By his word, Jesus rather gives a certain color to time: from now on, all time will be a chosen moment (a *kairos*). It is the quality of time that changes since from now on the Kingdom of God is imposed. Everything present will be much more than a simple moment on the timeline; it will be an occasion of commencing the Kingdom of God. As to knowing if such is effectively the case and understanding all that it can mean, that's what the rest of the narrative will have to reveal to the reader.

But Jesus' action likewise has a meaning for the future; the impact of his deeds and behavior is extended beyond death. It is in this way that the evangelist manages to riase the concern of all readers by what Jesus means, since they themselves live by definition in an age after Jesus' death. There are at least two aspects that make the scope of the story continue after Jesus' death. The first concerns the end of the Gospel in which the discovery of the empty tomb is narrated (Mark 16:1–8). This episode contains an explanation given by a young man dressed in white: Jesus has come back to life. The story of Jesus' personal life has not come to an end. But this event does not exist in itself. What happened to Jesus makes sense only through the command, addressed to the women who have stated that the tomb was empty, to tell the disciples to go to Galilee (Mark 16:7). The significance of the resurrection is only revealed in the later meeting with the disciples. In comparison with the other evangelists, Mark has this unique feature that even the text does not mention this meeting. Readers see themselves invested with an active and significant role in the completion of the story.

The second aspect is even more related to the destiny of people after Jesus' death. We find, especially in chapter 13 of the Gospel, a future perspective on the effect that Jesus can have on the world when people want to follow him. We call this speech of Jesus the "eschatological discourse" because the descriptions are associated with the end of time (*eschaton*). To decide to follow Jesus involves consequences. The disciples will be confronted with opponents because of the gospel. But there is more: the whole story and the cosmic movement are from now on interpreted as a consequence of what Jesus has provoked. Wars and famines, combats and earthquakes, false prophets and strange natural phenomena, solar and lunar eclipses . . . Everything that happens in the story after Jesus is a consequence of his action. This apocalyptic description of the times after Jesus, from the first years till the end of time, is a mixture of events on the earth and cosmic phenomena. Let's recall that in the ancients' conception of the world, the earth and the heavenly cosmos are bound one to the other. The dramatic character of chapter 13 can only be understood by taking account of this ancient cosmology. Thus we have to apply here also the rule of interpretation according to which apocalyptic language requires a "translation" for our age. It does not involve a literal description of what will happen on earth. Every effort to locate the concrete events of earthly history in a pre-established apocalyptic table can only be perverse. But by means of this game of mythological language, the narrator gets readers to find themselves confronted with a choice. This harsh language concerning the consequences of a choice for or against Jesus does not remain without an effect on readers. They get a clear idea of the fact that the decision to follow Jesus or not and to take seriously his gospel is in fact an existential question of life or death. Let's quote several verses as examples:

> Mark 13:9–23. "As for yourselves, beware; for they will hand you over to councils; and you will be beaten in synagogues; and you will stand before governors and kings because of me, as a testimony to them. And the good news must first be proclaimed to all nations. When they bring you to trial and hand you over, do not worry beforehand about what you are to say; but say whatever is given you at that time, for it is not you who speak, but the Holy Spirit. Brother will betray brother to death, and a father his child, and children will rise against parents and have them put to death; and you will be hated by all because of my name. But the one who endures to the end will be saved.
>
> "But when you see the desolating sacrilege set up where it ought not to be (let the reader understand) then those in Judea must flee to the mountains; the one on the housetop must not go down or

> enter the house to take anything away; the one in the field must not turn back to get a coat. Woe to those who are pregnant and to those who are nursing infants in those days! Pray that it may not be in winter. For in those days there will be suffering, such as has not been from the beginning of the creation that God created until now, no, and never will be. And if the Lord had not cut short those days, no one would be saved; but for the sake of the elect, whom he chose, he has cut short those days. And if anyone says to you at that time, 'Look! Here is the Messiah!' or 'Look! There he is!'—do not believe it. False messiahs and false prophets will appear and produce signs and omens, to lead astray, if possible, the elect. But be alert; I have already told you everything."

Promise and Fulfillment

The quotation ends with, "I have already told you everything." It is Jesus himself who proclaims the decisive significance of the gospel for the history of the world to come. This leads us to another literary aspect that serves the evangelist to orient his narrative. It is a matter of predictions, prophecies, and the promises of Jesus in which he announces what will happen after his death. This confers on him great authority. "I have already told you everything" is pronounced about the readers' era. It belongs to these readers to evaluate their own era in light of Jesus' words and to see if his predictions are confirmed. We find the same thing at the end of the gospel concerning the resurrection. These are the words that the women who came back to the tomb hear:

> Mark 16:7: But go, tell his disciples and Peter that he is going ahead of you to Galilee; there you will see him, *just as he told you.*

We are sent back thus explicitly to an earlier prediction of Jesus. We find it indeed a bit earlier in the text:

> Mark 14:27–28: And Jesus said to them, "You will all become deserters; for it is written, 'I will strike the shepherd, and the sheep will be scattered.' But after I am raised up, I will go before you to Galilee."

The narrator takes it up in a subtle way. He makes Jesus promise something and this promise is repeated by the young man near the tomb. This repetition of the promise already confirms that the words of Jesus have not been said in vain. The readers can consider this as a basis of confidence sufficient to believe that Jesus will actually go to Galilee. Although these same readers still need to examine whether this is indeed the case.

For them, these two examples are of such a nature to almost spontaneously sustain the question: "Can we trust the other strong promises about events that will occur beyond the limits of the text (resurrection and later passionate confrontations)? Can we believe that Jesus will rise from the dead and that his message determines the future of the world?" The answer is yes. But this trust is only possible because the narrator has done all he could to build as the plot goes on a relationship of trust with his readers. Other than the previously mentioned proceedings (omniscience of time and space) he comes to it equally by managing the pattern of "promise and fulfillment." The Gospel contains at different times an announcement in the form of a promise or prediction. And the narrator watches to show each time that the promise is fulfilled. The literary process of "promise and fulfillment" constitutes the basis from which readers can believe that Jesus' words about the resurrection and later developments will be actually fulfilled. This phenomenon equally seeks to create the greatest possible osmosis between a reliable narrator and the ideas and values of Jesus. Here are a few examples of this promise-fulfillment pattern:

1. One of the most developed cases is indubitably the prediction of the passion (and resurrection) by Jesus himself. As a glance at the structure of the Gospel clearly reveals, this case dominates the whole of the second part (see pp. 38–39). Jesus mentions his coming passion on different occasions. Here is the most elaborated text:

> Mark 10:32b–34: He took the twelve aside again and began to tell them what was to happen to him, saying, "See, we are going up to Jerusalem, and the Son of Man will be handed over to the chief priests and the scribes, and they will condemn him to death; then they will hand him over to the Gentiles; they will mock him, and spit upon him, and flog him, and kill him; and after three days he will rise again."

In the course of the Passion itself, the elements making part of this prediction will appear again almost scrupulously. We will be satisfied here with mentioning the realization of a few parts only of the prediction:

- The betrayal by Judas:

> Mark 14:18b-21: Jesus said, "Truly I tell you, one of you will betray me, one who is eating with me." They began to be distressed and to

> say to him one after another, "Surely, not I?" He said to them, "It is one of the twelve, one who is dipping bread into the bowl with me. For the Son of Man goes as it is written of him, but woe to that one by whom the Son of Man is betrayed! It would have been better for that one not to have been born."

- The mockery scene in all its details:

> Mark 15:17–20: And they clothed him in a purple cloak; and after twisting some thorns into a crown, they put it on him. And they began saluting him, "Hail, King of the Jews!" They struck his head with a reed, spat upon him, and knelt down in homage to him. After mocking him, they stripped him of the purple cloak and put his own clothes on him. Then they led him out to crucify him.

- Even death:

> Mark 15:37: Then Jesus gave a loud cry and breathed his last.

Thanks to an exact account of the realization of Jesus' prediction, readers have confidence in the power and assurance of this man. This is a superb example in which form and content are in complete sync. The picture of Jesus is drawn by the rhetorical talent of the narrator: all the authorities join in their opposition to Jesus, but he continues to master the setting of his near death himself.

2. In order to again reinforce the feeling of the authority of Jesus on the readers, the evangelist does not limit his promise-fulfillment pattern to an isolated case. He gives more samples of remarkable predictions that are fulfilled. As, for example, the order to the disciples to find a donkey when Jesus approaches Jerusalem. Here is the text:

> Mark 11:1–6: When they were approaching Jerusalem, at Bethphage and Bethany, near the Mount of Olives, he sent two of his disciples and said to them, "Go into the village ahead of you, and immediately as you enter it, you will find tied there a colt that has never been ridden; untie it and bring it. If anyone says to you, 'Why are you doing this?' just say this, 'The Lord needs it and will send it back here immediately.'" They went away and found a colt tied near a door, outside in the street. As they were untying it, some of the bystanders said to them, "What are you doing, untying the colt?" They told them what Jesus had said; and they allowed them to take it.

Once again, readers do not have to let themselves be deceived by thinking that it is a matter here of a historical reproduction of an exceptional paranormal gift of Jesus. No, the evangelist emphasizes Jesus' authority. It is thus not by accident that verse 6 says explicitly, "They said as Jesus had said," accentuating Jesus' role in the whole.

3. The order or the mission of the disciples to find a room in Jerusalem to celebrate the Passover is almost identical. They had to follow a man carrying a jug of water in order that he could lead them to a large upstairs room. The text says thus:

> Mark 14:16: So the disciples set out and went to the city, and found everything as he had told them.

4. The betrayal by Judas like Peter's denials is equally the object of predictions. It is enough to compare verses 14:30 and 14:72:

> Mark 14:30: Jesus said to him, "Truly I tell you, this day, this very night, before the cock crows twice, you will deny me three times.

> Mark 14:72: At the moment the cock cried for the second time. Then Peter remembered that Jesus had said to him, "Before the cock crows twice, you will deny me three times."

5. These are only a few examples. Perhaps we can again see in the general warning of the previously mentioned eschatological discourse a kind of prediction, notably that the disciples will not be able to watch during Jesus' last night:

> Mark 13:36–37: [. . .] or else he may find you asleep when he comes suddenly. And what I say to you, I say to all: Keep awake!

> Mark 14:37: He came and found them sleeping; and he said to Peter: "Simon, are you asleep? Could you not keep awake one hour?"

Doublets in the Gospel

The "promise and fulfillment" pattern that repeats what has first of all been predicted is only one example among many others of a much larger literary phenomenon that makes Mark's reputation. We also find "doublets" in the text. If the term "doublet" is applied to several areas, it will designate here one or the other kind of repetition or elaboration of a text in two stages. Doublets are much more remarkable when pericopes, brief passages, or entire sentences are repeated (almost) word for word, which we observe best by reading or hearing the Gospel as a whole. We cannot avoid them when there are two miracle stories about a small quantity of bread multiplied for thousands of people (Mark 6:34–44; 8:1–9). Or when there are two healings of a blind man (Mark 8:22–26; 10:46–52). Likewise, we find the description of the tempest on the lake in the narrative in which Jesus calms precisely this tempest and in the passage in which Jesus walks on the water (Mark 4:35–41; 6:45–52). It is still the same when, in almost identical terms, speculation about Jesus' identity unfolds: Is it John the Baptist who has come back, Elijah, or another prophet (Mark 6:14–16; 8:27–28)? It is not by chance either if Jesus is twice questioned, first by the Jewish authorities (Mark 14:55–65) and a second time by the Roman governor, Pontius Pilate (Mark 15:1–15).

Sometimes, the narrator seeks to show readers in a particular way that two stories, apparently without any connection, can nevertheless be brought into harmony. He does it by slipping one of the stories into the other, which we sometimes call a "sandwich" construction. We know six clearly established cases, but I will limit myself here to four of them. We cannot, for example, *not* bring the criticisms of those near Jesus into harmony with the accusations uttered by the scribes who had come from Jerusalem (Mark 3:20–21, 22–30, 31–35). Likewise, it is perfectly clear that the narrator has inserted the healing of the woman with a flow of blood between the introduction and the conclusion of the story of the healing of the little daughter of Jairus (Mark 5:21–24, 25–34, 35–43). The murder of John the Baptist, which is obviously meant to fill in the time between the mission of the apostles and their return, invites readers to dig deeper to find a connection between these stories: Could the fate of John prefigure that of the disciples of Jesus, even of Jesus himself (Mark 6:7–13, 14–29, 30)? The insertion of Peter's denials into the story of the interrogation of Jesus by the Jewish Sanhedrin gives an extraordinary dramatic power to the two stories. Whereas Jesus is quiet and lets himself be humiliated, the eminent disciple Peter cannot stop himself at the same time from denying that he knows Christ three times (Mark 14:54, 55–65, 66–72).

More Doublets

Once readers realize that Mark favors this genre of repetitions or stories in two stages, they understand that the Gospel is in fact full of this stylistic procedure. We also recognize doublets in the text at a more simple level. Indeed we can draw up a list of examples in which the evangelist tells one thing in his narrative that will be confirmed in the words uttered by Jesus or by another person. Technically, we call this "narrative and discourse," i.e., tradition or stories *about* Jesus taken up through the discursive tradition (or words *of* Jesus). In the following examples, this is indicated by an arrow.

> Mark 5:38: [. . .] he saw a commotion, people weeping and wailing loudly. → 39: When he had entered, he said to them: "Why do you make a commotion and weep?"

> Mark 6:32: And they went away in the boat to a deserted place by themselves. [. . .] 35: When it grew late, his disciples came to him and said, → "This is a deserted place, and the hour is now very late."

> Mark 8:16: They said to one another, "It is because we have no bread." → 17: And becoming aware of it, Jesus said to them: "Why are you talking about having no bread?"

I want to draw attention to another specific example of doublets. There are cases in which they serve to create a close unity between the narrator's thought and that of Jesus. Jesus gives an order and the narrator takes up almost the same words to relate that the order has been carried out. A few examples:

> Mark 6:7: He called the twelve and began to send them out two by two, and gave them authority over the unclean spirits. → 6:12–13: So they went out and proclaimed that all should repent. They cast out many demons [. . .].

> Mark 4:39a: He woke up and rebuked the wind, and said to the sea, "Peace! Be still!" → 4:39b Then the wind ceased, and there was a dead calm.

It also happens that Jesus is asked a question, the words of which he takes up in his reply.

> Mark 1:40: [A leper] came to him begging him, and [kneeling] he said to him, "If you choose, you can make me clean."→ 41: Jesus

> [. . .] stretched out his hand [. . .] and said to him, "I do choose. Be made clean."

> Mark 5:28: For she said, "If I but touch his clothes, I will be made well." → 34: He said to her, "Daughter, your faith has made you well; go in peace, and be healed of your disease."

We also find certain explanations in the narrative in which the narrator and the protagonist express an identical opinion. Mark's reaction to the disciples' lack of understanding is a characteristic example.

> Mark 6:51b–52: [The voice of the evangelist] And they were utterly astounded, for they did not understand about the loaves, but their hearts were hardened. → 8:17 [Jesus' voice] "Why are you talking about having no bread? Do you still not perceive or understand? Are your hearts hardened?" [. . .] 8:21: Then he said to them, "Do you not yet understand?"

In all these cases, it is a matter of sentences or turns of phrases taken up by repetition. But there are still dozens of other small grammatical or literary aspects in the text in which we recognize doublets. An exhaustive glance at these even smaller phenomena would however take us much too far [see Bibliography]. My only intention is to invite readers to keep a lookout for certain aspects during the reading of the Gospel by furnishing in each case one or two examples, without losing sight that there are probably hundreds of them to point to:

- Double indication of time:

> Mark 1:32: That evening, at sundown . . .

> Mark 1:35: In the morning, while it was still very dark . . .

- Double indication of place:

> Mark 5:14: The swineherds [. . .] told it in the city and in the country . . .

> Mark 11:11: Then he entered Jerusalem and went into the temple . . .

- Double participle:

Mark 1:14–15: Jesus came to Galilee, *proclaiming* the good news of God and *saying* . . .

Mark 8:11: The Pharisees came and began to argue with him, *asking* him for a sign from heaven and *testing* him.

- Double commandment:

Mark 4:39: He woke up and rebuked the wind, and said to the sea: "*Peace! Be still!*"

Mark 8:15: And he cautioned them, saying, "*Watch out—beware of the yeast of the Pharisees and the yeast of Herod.*"

Mark 10:49: And they called the blind man, saying to him, "*Take heart; get up*, he is callling you."

Specialists have observed that the phenomenon of repetition is present equally at the most minute grammatical level in the Greek text. There are at least seventy examples in which the preposition in the compound verb is taken up. Translations naturally avoid this phenomenon, as a verbatim rendition might read, for example:

Mark 6:54: When they left (out) of the boat

Mark 9:43: It would better for you to enter (into) armless into life . . .

The Importance of Doublets

At the end of this long passage on doublets, readers perhaps may question the reasons for this broad explanation. Why so much insistence on the phenomenon of doublets? We will return later to the consequences at the level of the contents of a few concrete repetitions (for example, the two multiplications of bread). But the first significance of our approach to all these doublets is perhaps only understood by a brief backward glance at the history of scholarship on Mark. For a longtime, these doublets have aroused a hypothesis that consisted of dividing the Gospel into different sources or strata. Doublets would constitute proof that the evangelist had joined several textual sources into a single text. This witnesses to a completely different vision about the author of the Gospel than in the narrative method. The author loses his status as linguistic artist and becomes a kind of collector of texts turning the original fragments in a more or less clever way into an incoherent whole. The idea inevitably implies that, by this copy-paste approach, the evangelist obscured Jesus' original meaning. It has as a consequence given way to a true hunt for treasure, namely, an early text of the Gospel that would reveal Jesus' true nature. In the first half of the twentieth century, scholars succeeded in dividing the Gospel into two or three sources by reducing the contribution of the evangelist to an occasional word. In the narrative approach doublets are a proof to the contrary. Their constant usage reveals the hand of a unique narrator. No question of the careless redaction of the text or of collection of fragments emerging in a general impression of confusion! Readers can thus trust their impression that the author is completely worthy of confidence. But this vision of the evangelist is possible only if we admit and radically recognize that an author has the right to recover history with the veil of his subjective vision. This "knowledge" that the evangelist communicates about his principle character, Jesus, is a personal interpretation of the author.

In Mark, this conception of a "gospel" is supported in a tangible way by the coherence of his style. Doublets do not always have the same function. We have just seen a much different nature. They sometimes function to surround a passage, sometimes they consciously repeat to insist on a point, sometimes again they simplify the reading by repetition. But all together, they arouse in readers the impression of being face-to-face with an author who has created a completely coherent work.

Doublets have for a second effect that, beyond the narrator, Jesus also appears as a character worthy of trust. Through repetition, numerous words of the evangelist are parallel to those of Jesus, which creates the impression that the author and Jesus share the same vision of events. The same words suggest the same values

Summaries

Does the author use yet other rhetorical features in his aim to transmit the picture of Jesus to his readers? For a long time scholarship has been reluctant to settle on general or synthesizing descriptions—the so-called *summaria* or summaries. Most of the pericopes in the Gospel in effect describe individual events linked to a person, a place, and a specific time as, for example, the healing of a blind person, Jesus' discourse at the edge of the lake, or the call of the twelve on a mountain. More than a general description, the specificity of the event gives more vivacity and tension to the pericope at hand and it functions therefore better in liturgy. The Gospel thus gives the readers a concrete impression. Jesus is near each particular person and the personal meeting with Jesus occupies the central place. Readers cannot fail to feel this. But at dozens of places, especially in the first part of the Gospel, the narrator abandons this anecdotal style to insert one or several verses that take up and resume what is happening in more general terms. It is very characteristic for Mark to do it from the beginning of the Gospel. It will therefore suffice here to illustrate Mark's use of summaries by focusing on the first chapter of his Gospel. Let's recall, however, that we are alluding to a meaning in which the form of the gospel (the *how*) is its content (the *what*). We can also discern this phenomenon in the summaries.

The first summary concerning Jesus picks up his first words:

> Mark 1:14–15: Now after John was arrested, Jesus came to Galilee, proclaiming the good news of God, and saying, "The time is fulfilled, and the kingdom of God has come near; repent, and believe in the good news."

A lively mind will immediately understand that these words are certainly not the first that Jesus pronounced in public. There is not even a single person present to hear this solemn declaration of Jesus. But this summary that figures in the beginning of the Gospel marvelously presents Jesus and his message and gives a tone to everything that follows. All that Jesus does and says must be interpreted in the light of the coming of the Kingdom of God and everything that will follow is "good news" or "gospel." We could almost consider that the gospel is constituted so to speak, from footnotes at the bottom of the page for this initial program of Jesus. The only real auditors of these first words of Jesus are the readers or the audience who have to constantly remember when they will be informed more about this person. Anticipating the following, we can now affirm that not only the miracles and parables are part of the gospel, but that, according to Mark, even the passion and the death of Jesus are part of the good news!

The second summary is in the setting of the first liberating intervention of Jesus, the healing of a possessed man in the synagogue. This action is followed by the words:

> Mark 1:28: At once his fame began to spread throughout the surrounding region of Galilee.

The narrator's intention in this verse is obvious. His main character is made known as someone extraordinary. He is truly special and from his first act, the impression that he leaves is unforgettable. The effect on readers also is undeniable: this person is worth the effort that we have to make to accompany him. The summary that follows almost immediately moreover provokes an identical result. After having performed the above mentioned exorcism in the synagogue and having healed Simon's mother-in-law—thus after merely two miracles—the evangelist shifts to another linguistic level to tell us:

> Mark 1:32–34: That evening, at sundown, they brought to him all who were sick or possessed with demons. And the whole city was gathered around the door. And he cured many who were sick with various diseases, and cast out many demons; and he would not permit the demons to speak, because they knew him.

These verses make up a new summary and suggest that Jesus' action meets a rapid success. They stress two kinds of action: exorcisms and healings. It is obviously once again an interpretation on the part of the narrator. In a few words Mark alludes to a picture of Jesus with many facets. Here are some of them: Jesus is liberator and healer, he is available to all, his fight is against evil at all levels (illnesses and demons). The fact that the narrator insists so explicitly on this first picture of Jesus as liberator determines what readers should retain about this man. Readers will indeed be confronted all along the first part of the Gospel with a Jesus who heals people and who delivers them. In order to reinforce this picture, the evangelist inserts between the individual anecdotes general descriptions of a Jesus healing many sick people and delivering the possessed. In fact, through these summaries it is his own profession of faith that the narrator proposes to the readers: the evangelist sees in these healings and these exorcisms how Jesus transposes the gospel into acts. The unceasing repetition and generalizations are intended to leave an indelible impression on the readers.

By adding the three summaries mentioned above, Jesus shows himself as someone who announces the good news (Mark 1:14–15) by acting (Mark 1:32–34) successfully (Mark 1:28). This is the picture that readers can carry away from this first chapter of Mark. It will therefore be a beautiful story bringing good news in which people are healed and delivered and all this thanks to Jesus. It is thus not surprising that the narrator inserts another two summaries almost one after another that are focused on the impact of Jesus:

> Mark 1:39: And he went throughout Galilee, proclaiming the message in their synagogues and casting out demons.
>
> Mark 1:45: [. . .] and people came to him from every quarter.

Other Stylistic Characteristics

Our attention is again drawn by other aspects of Mark's style: the use of irony or preferential words or anticipation of future events or the reference back to earlier events. We will have to be content however only to mention here a single characteristic. Form and content are manifestly bound together in the frequent use of references to the Old Testament or to quotations from the latter. Mark makes quotations from the Torah, from the prophets, and psalms by using them for multiple purposes. They can, for example, designate the identity of Jesus. Thus from the going up to Jerusalem, the text says:

> Mark 11:9–10: Then those who went ahead and those who followed were shouting, "Hosanna! Blessed is the one who comes in the name of the Lord! Blessed is the coming kingdom of our ancestor David! Hosanna in the highest heaven!" (Ps 118:25–26).

And Jesus indisputably alludes to himself when he says:

> Mark 12:10–11: Have you not read this scripture: "The stone that the builders rejected has become the cornerstone; this was the Lord's doing, and it is amazing in our eyes"? (Ps 118:22–23).

The Scriptures also serve as a means of proving that Jesus is a better exegete than his opponents. In his discussions with the scribes, Jesus at each turn concludes the controversy to his advantage. He goes so far even to reprimand the scribes by basing himself on arguments from Scripture. I give two examples only:

> Mark 7:6–8: He said to them, "Isaiah prophesied rightly about you hypocrites, as it is written, 'This people honors me with their lips, but their hearts are far from me; in vain do they worship me,

> teaching human precepts as doctrines.' You abandon the commandment of God and hold to human tradition."

> Mark 10:3–5: He answered them, "What did Moses command you?" They said, "Moses allowed a man to write a certificate of dismissal and to divorce her." But Jesus said to them, "Because of your hardness of heart he wrote this commandment for you.

Considerations about the Evangelist's Rhetoric

To conclude, I am eager to place these considerations about the narrator's rhetoric in the general context of this book. The analysis presupposed that all the readers feel challenged by the signals emitted by the text and that they react to it. Whether or not to dispose of important scholarly knowledge about the Gospel or to read the book in an ecclesiastical or faith context is not at all the order of the day. I want only to demonstrate how this work functions at the literary level. It is through the rhetoric of the narrator that all readers come in contact with their vision about Jesus. Rhetoric teaches us that what we read is not an objective account of what historically happened. The Gospel is the account of the narrator's opinion. And precisely because it is a matter of a personal interpretation, this narrative constitutes a basis and an invitation to dialogue between the story told and the readers. Let's briefly repeat some of the narrator's points of view: Jesus is liberator and healer and his significance is of decisive importance for history. Likewise we have understood that the author is a person of his own time when he uses mythical language, which appears from time to time in his understanding of the cosmos or in his way of allowing transcendent beings an active role in the affairs on the earth. If it is no longer possible today to use this view of the world, the author's idea has not at all changed: Jesus has an exceptional significance. The narrator strives moreover by all means not to present Jesus as a mythical person. He is on the contrary a being of flesh and blood. In the texts quoted, Jesus does not claim for himself a divine status. That's why in the following chapter we will elaborate on the intercourse between Jesus and God and more particularly on the expression "Son of God."

In speaking of the mythical language that Mark uses, let's come back for a moment to the question of knowing whether or not we have to have faith to read the Gospel. More concretely, mythical language raises the very question of what it means to "have faith." For some people, to have faith indeed implies that we hold to a specific use of the language. The difference between believer and unbeliever then comes down to whether or not we admit a mythico-religious language as truth. In Mark, we find this language in the words of Jesus about the fate of the disciples and the world after his death. We also find it in the presence of demons in possessed people. But our analysis well shows that this language cannot be separated from its era and that it cannot be taken in a woodenly literal way. Mythical language needs a "translation." Besides, the reading of Mark does not stir up the impression that even the evangelist orients the discussion to faith, in a specific discourse in mythological language. In faith it is a matter of other things, above all of the way of seeing Jesus. When we meet the term "faith" (*pistis* in Greek) in Mark, four times it is in a context of healing and once in a context of prayer. Here are the texts. Only a single occurrence appears in which it is said what we must "have faith" in (in God).

> Mark 2:5: When Jesus saw their *faith*, he said to the paralytic, "Son, your sins are forgiven."

> Mark 4:40: He said to them, "Why are you afraid? Have you still no *faith*?"

> Mark 5:34: He said to her, "Daughter, your faith has made you well; go in peace and be healed of your disease."

> Mark 10:52: Jesus said to him, "Go, your *faith* has made you well." Immediately he regained his sight and followed him on the way.

> Mark 11:22: Jesus answered them, "Have *faith* in God."

Ten times we find the verb "believe," likewise in contexts of healing or prayer and once with an object (Mark 1:15: believe in the gospel). It seems therefore that, much more than believing in one or another linguistic list, it is important to have trust basically in what Jesus does (heal) or in what God can do (prayer). This said, this last part is not concretized either, but we find it in the form of a metaphor:

> Mark 11:23: "Truly I tell you, if you say to this mountain, 'Be taken up and thrown into the sea,' and if you do not doubt in your heart, but believe that what you say will come to pass, it will be done for you."

Whatever the case may be, Mark's readers do not escape the impression that Jesus is really the central character, that he is what the Gospel is all about. To believe means then, to leave the field free to Jesus to heal or to cast out the demons, so that he can do what he has to do. All that is the good news (= gospel). Do you have to have faith to read the Gospel? That seems to be an almost anachronistic question without the slightest affinity with Mark's readers. Through the reading of the Gospel, the question is quite simply reversed: the way to see Jesus is basically a question of faith. His story defies each one of us, believers and unbelievers, to define more clearly for ourselves what our relationship to Jesus is.

Up to this point, the recall of healing stories and summaries has mostly spoken to us of Jesus' successes. In this sense, it is not so difficult for the readers and spectators of his time to have a positive view of Jesus. But what follows is not so simple. In ending this part on the rhetoric of the evangelist, it is good to pass to the content of the Gospel. The last time that the evangelist uses the verb "believe" in the Gospel, he does it in a quite specific context. Jesus is on the cross and is mocked by some of the spectators. The passage ends with "so that we may see and believe." Here it is:

> Mark 15:31–32: In the same way the chief priests, along with the scribes, were also mocking him among themselves and saying, "He saved others; he cannot save himself. Let the Messiah, the King of Israel, come down from the cross now, so that we may see and believe."

These last words are charged with irony. In just these few words, the evangelist makes all the tension of the Gospel appear. The conflict has ended and the authorities have Jesus executed. Jesus' prophetic words about his own crucifixion have been realized. They mock him as he had predicted. But one of the predictions expressed on several occasions by Jesus remains unaccomplished up to now: Will he rise from among the dead? Has everything finished for the Crucified One? Or not? The mockers seem to have it all their own way and feel themselves in a position of strength. It is conquerors who write history. And the death of a person puts an end to their story. They are convinced that they have finished with Jesus. But their words about the verb "believe" appear ironic in the eyes of readers in the light of the prophecy that the evangelist has left open:

> Mark 9:9–10: As they were coming down the mountain, he ordered them to tell no one about what they had seen, until after the Son of Man had risen from the dead. So they kept the matter

to themselves, questioning what this rising from the dead could mean.

Until now, our approach has been limited to unveiling the mechanisms by which that narrative takes its strength. For the readers it is still too early to make decisions, but they have in every way been enabled to avoid an eventual misunderstanding: the narrative does not give an objective account of historical facts of which everybody could be convinced as if it were a mathematical argument. Mark's Gospel expresses the personal vision of an author who is persuaded that Jesus has a decisive significance for all who find themselves in his presence. This is the point of departure to begin to read the Gospel. From then on, the question is, "What do readers understand about the *content* of the narrative?"

Bibliography

Fowler, R. M. *Loaves* and *Fishes. The Function of the Feeding Stories in the Gospel of Mark.* SBL Diss 54. Chico, CA: Scholars, 1984 (on the function of "doublets" in the Gospel according to Mark).

Marguerat, D., and Y. Bourquin. *Pour lire les récits bibliques.* 4th ed. Paris: Labor et Fides, 2009.

Neirynck, F. Duality *in Mark: Contributions to the Study of the Markan Redaction.* 2nd ed. Bibliotheca Ephemeridum Theologicarum Lovaniensium 31. Louvain: University Press, 1988 (complete catalogue of thirty categories of all the forms of "duality" in the gospel according to Mark).

Rhoads, D., J. Dewey, and D. Michie. *Mark as Story: An Introduction to the Narrative of a Gospel.* 2nd ed. Minneapolis: Fortress, 1999 (narratological analysis of Mark with much interest for the style of the evangelist).

Segovia, F., and M. A. Tolbert, eds. *Social Location and Biblical Interpretation in the Global Perspective.* Vol. 2 of *Reading from This Place.* Minneapolis: Fortress, 1995 (on the way reading of the Bible is determined by the social context).

Van Oyen, G. *De summaria in Marcus en de compositie van Mc 1,14–8,26.* SNTA 12; Louvain: Peeters, 1987 (the summaries in the Gospel according to Mark).

———. "Intercalation and Irony in the Gospel of Mark." In *The Four Gospels*, edited by F. Van Segbroeck, C. M. Tuckett, J. Verheyden, and G. Van Belle, 2:949–74. Bibliotheca Ephemeridum Theologicarum Lovaniensium 100; Festschrift Frans Neirynck. Louvain: Peeters, 1992.

———. "Repetitious Style and the Interpretation of the Gospel of Mark." In *Repetitions and Variations in the Fourth Gospel*, edited by G. Van Belle, M. Labahn and P. Maritz, 109–25. Bibliotheca Ephemeridum Theologicarum Lovaniensium 223. Louvain: Peeters, 2009.

5

Jesus with a Question Mark

THIS CHAPTER SHOULD MAKE us advance in the content of Mark's Gospel. Let's plunge directly to the essential. And this for a quite simple reason: the objective is to get a perfectly clear picture of the general impression of the main theme that Mark proposes to his readers. Then, I will place all the other ideas or questions in this setting. By operating differently, we risk banging into small obstacles in the text that prevent us from getting through to what is essential. It seems to me that the central question is: How does the picture that the evangelist makes of Jesus' identity reach the readers? Who is Jesus? This question truly plunges into the heart of the Gospel. The exact manner of evaluating this picture is to attentively read the Gospel from the beginning to the end. Most of the time, we come into contact with the Gospel by reading or studying it, or again through the liturgy, but almost always through relatively brief passages. This never allows us to see the big narrative course appear. It is only by impregnating ourselves with the grand whole that we come to suspect something of the dynamic and the tension that the evangelist wanted to communicate.

Reading in Reality

Our proposal is to analyze here the process of the readers' experience with the character Jesus. Through the analysis of this experience of the readers themselves, we discover the way the evangelist operates who endeavors to communicate his picture of Jesus to the readers. The idea that sustains the process of the narrative analysis is that only the text makes possible the meeting with the picture of Jesus proposed by Mark. Literary theories have produced, among others, a model allowing us to represent the communication between an author and his readers. We suppose, as a starting point, that there is a *real author* (the evangelist) and *real readers* of flesh and blood (the original targeted group). But they are not with us any longer and they remain moreover illustrious unknowns. This we could regret, because we could have asked them many questions so as to enlighten us about the first interpretations of the Gospel. In the absence of the real author and the first readers, literary theory has created two completely new ideas: an implied author and an implied reader or a group of implied readers. Both of them are imaginary realities. The *implied author* corresponds to the picture of the author we get from the text. In fact, this creation says nothing more than that: it is possible to reconstruct from the text an author and readers who are the reflection one of the other and who send (the author) or receive (readers) a maximum of corresponding signals. Such a reconstructed picture is however an inaccessible ideal because the signals of a text are, if not indefinitely, at least extremely numerous. But, at least, these concepts of implied author and reader(s) presuppose that we keep our minds largely open in the interpretation of the text. Interpretation is never finished. The text remains a permanent invitation to interpretation. Each new reading is capable of revealing things we did not take account of before. My personal opinion is that the role of the *implied readers* is largely determined by the real readers of the moment, that is to say, me or all other possible readers of the Gospel. Each individual reader engaged with the text creates an *implied author and implied reader(s)* with their own possibilities and difficulties. For me, the *implied reader* does not exist in the singular. He is composed of numerous constructions elaborated by so many real readers. This is why the role of real readers is always the most important for the explanation of the text.

Let's abandon this theoretical model, recalling what it involves: it has the merit of putting us on guard against a too naive reading to the text, as if we were friends with the author and the original readers. For interested readers, I briefly review here the schema spelled out by Bas van Iersel in his *Reading Mark*. In comparison with existing literary models, it has, in my opinion, two advantages. On the one hand, van Iersel reverses the orientation of the way in which the interpretation of the message takes place. Even if that can seem paradoxical, interpretation does not begin with the author's intention. The power of imagination of the readers is what takes the initiative. On the other hand, what is interpreted is the picture that the *real* readers (and not the implied reader constructed in a purely theoretical way) are imagining of the text. From there arises the importance of the big arrow to the right side of the schema:

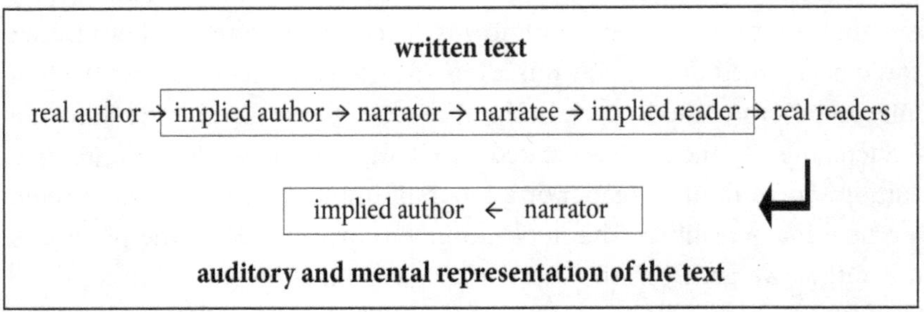

The Exegete as a Guide, the Text and the Reader

In the final account it is important for what follows that the readers of this book and I know that it is not a question here of one single process of reading. The exegete's task is to try to be a guide for the reader. Just as the function of a tour guide is to make a work of art or an edifice appear in all their glory, the exegete is to act in the same way. As a guide, the exegete also tells his perspective about the narrative. He proposes a possible way to read. Guides interpret, they have their own history, and insert personal accents in their explanations. They explain in their own way that there is a seductive power in the text or the work of art. The beauty of a painting or a monument is accessible to every person. And each one feels this beauty by the colors and the lines of a painting, the shapes of a sculpture, or the proportions of a building. Whether an architect or an art historian explains the origin of the work, the symbolism of the different colors or attributes, the materials used, or the placement of a statue, all that takes nothing away from that first experience. On the contrary, these explanations dialogue with the first impressions. Sometimes, they are deepened, sometimes contradicted and yet sometimes, new perspectives are born that allow us to test and admire the beauty in a more intense way. It is in this way that a personal and conscious vision of the spectator is formed. And that's what it is all about in the end. But let's observe first of all two aspects of the

Gospel's work of art: the numerous questions raised in the Gospel (chap. 5) and scruples over the use of the titles given to Jesus (chap. 6).

The First Experience of Reading: Under a Flood of Questions

The reader who reads through the Gospel from the beginning to the end is confronted with problems. Questions arise about the meaning of characters and/or events. There are so many "gaps" in the story, in which the text seems to wait for the reader to call on his own creativity to fill in the meaning. But what is remarkable in Mark is that the narrator creates a kind of solidarity between the text and the questions of the reader. He in fact does things so that one of the salient parts of his text is precisely to constantly insert *questions*. We have counted more than a hundred and ten examples. It is a characteristic consciously inserted by the evangelist in order to make his readers reflect. If the narrator asks so many questions, the readers must no longer be surprised that for them there also remain questions. Most of these questions concern the person of Jesus. The impression that's created is obvious: Jesus is someone who arouses questions in his wake. And the questioning look that the readers ask about Jesus is the same as that of the spectators of their time. We can say in general terms that something about Jesus—what he does and says—causes people in the narrative who have contact with him to seek to know more about him, or to show themselves critical or full of lack of understanding of him. Below are some of these questions, but let's note already that the questioners are very diverse: there are the opponents of Jesus, but also his disciples, his family, his judges, the sick, or the demons who cross his path. Let's look first at the questions coming from his different opponents.

First Question: A Demon

The questions from a first meeting in the synagogue with a possessed person directly give the tone for what follows.

> Mark 1:21–28: They went to Capernaum; and when the sabbath came, he entered the synagogue and taught. They were astounded at his teaching, for he taught them as one having authority, and not as the scribes. Just then there was in their synagogue a man with an unclean spirit, and he cried out, "What have you to do with

> us, Jesus of Nazareth? Have you come to destroy us? I know who you are, the Holy One of God." But Jesus rebuked him, saying, "Be silent, and come out of him!" And the unclean spirit, convulsing him and crying with a loud voice, came out of him. They were all amazed, and they kept on asking one another, "What is this? A new teaching—with authority! He commands even the unclean spirits, and they obey him." At once his fame began to spread throughout the surrounding region of Galilee.

The demon recognizes Jesus at the same moment he asks, full of astonishment, why Jesus would have the intention of destroying him. He even says in the plural, "to destroy us." The discussion is not fortuitous but fundamental. Jesus dares to confront extra-human forces. It is a classic fact of the stories of exorcism that a battle for power bursts out between the demon and the exorcist. One of the strategies used to get the victory is to try to unmask the identity of the adversary so as not to be taken by him. But the demon in this story does not succeed in his quest and hollows out in some way his own tomb by recognizing Jesus as the Holy One of God. It can seem strange to our contemporaries that the narrator does not focus his attention on the problem that generally intrigues modern people, that is to say, the functioning of such an exorcism. And it is true that it is not so much the narrator's problem. In the presentation of things in this era, demons quite simply exist and it was quite possible to exorcize them. For the real theme of this narrative we have to go in another direction. The narrator is concerned in fact to know why Jesus expends his power to deliver a possessed person. He wants readers to ask themselves what is the extent of the power of this remarkable person and to do this he introduces a comparison between Jesus and other possessors of power. Indeed readers see a readymade meaning of this first miracle: on two occasions the spectators, at the same time stunned and admiring, state that this man Jesus is someone who speaks and acts with authority and they have not yet seen anything like it. There are of course many other people of authority, but their competence is limited to the Scriptures. In Jesus, they see someone who, moreover, acts with effectiveness and casts out unclean spirits.

If the affirmation that Jesus teaches with authority is striking, it is also quite striking that we do not find a word about the contents of his teaching. Or rather, the content of his teaching is precisely Jesus' action that frees the possessed person. Other passages in the Gospel closely associate the acts of Jesus to his words. When a little later Jesus, observing the crowd, sees it like sheep without a shepherd, he takes pity and begins to teach them (Mark

6:34). But another time, not a word about what he teaches. What follows is the well-known story of Jesus who feeds five thousand people by distributing five loaves and two fish (Mark 6:35–44). And the narrator insists on the fact that the words of Jesus are equivalent to his acts. He does what he says.

The importance of these first questions in the Gospel (both those of the demons and those of the spectators) is that they reveal that everything that Jesus does and says is placed in the context of power and authority. What Jesus does, calls forth admiration because it is, in all its radicalness, a demonstration of power. These questions express very clearly that he does not avoid conflict. We have seen above that this conflict unfolds at two levels. This is already the case at this first healing of a person possessed by a demon. The intervention of Jesus is located in the tangible and felt reality of life. That's the first dimension of his action. We observe that he has the power to restore health to someone. His message from the first *summary* (Mark 1:14–15) concerning the coming of the Kingdom of God is for the first time seen here concretized. It is not a rule outside of the real world. Neither is it distant or disembodied. But an exorcism inevitably implies a second dimension, because it is also a fight at the transcendent level. It is not at his own doing that Jesus casts out demons, but because he is the Holy One *of God*. The demon, which symbolizes evil dominating a human being inexplicably, can only be destroyed by a power that also transcends the human. The first act of deliverance performed by Jesus is a natural consequence of what he has previously lived during his solitary stay in the desert. He had fought for forty days with Satan and . . . conquered him. This anecdote should directly warn the reader that Jesus is sustained by God and that he is able to conquer evil.

Through his way of describing the first public act of Jesus, the narrator somewhat abandons his readers through several considerations. Here are two of them. First, does Jesus really hold his power from God? And what sort of God is this that everyone so marvels at Jesus' action? And will there be other conflicts and who then will be the adversaries? They are two considerations of a different order. To find the answer to the second question about conflicts, it is enough to envisage the development in what follows in the Gospel. But the first consideration, that about the function of God, presupposes that the reader makes a decision. Indeed it is a question about the significance of God that is usually asked in this form: Is God really at work in Jesus? This formulation presupposes that one already has formed an idea of God and that from that will verify whether this picture is also applied in an adequate way to Jesus. But I take here for a moment the role of a reading guide for the rest of this book by taking up the question again in a different way. Is it really indicated that we should integrate the action of Jesus as a part of a picture of God to construct? In asking the question in this way, the acts of Jesus become a challenge addressed to the readers' picture of God. Must we, can we, or do we want to recognize God in what Jesus does?

A new formulation of the connection between Jesus and God is completely suitable to this book, which seeks not universally proposed conceptions but respect for the plurality of readers. Beginning with the acts and words of Jesus, these readers see themselves urged to reflect on a possible image of God. The Gospel seems to presuppose this questioning. The text is supported by the person of Jesus as he acts and speaks. It is obvious that our time is different from that of Mark, in which religion, God, divinities, and the divine being were part of the evidences of the common life. It is thus normal to make this relation between the action of Jesus and God relevant for our own time. We will mention later the Jewish and Hellenistic places that constitute the necessary context to understand the interpretations of Jesus in the Gospels. But the cultural differences between this revolutionary era and ours in no way forbid that Mark's question can still always be asked in the same way: What is the image of God that is created by the facts and deeds of Jesus?

Second Question: The Scribes

When for the second time Jesus is questioned about his acts, we make the acquaintance of the scribes, people who will become later in the Gospel his more and more stubborn opponents. Their presence is not unexpected because at the preceding confrontation, the spectators have already perceived that Jesus' vision does not really coincide with that of the scribes.

> Mark 2:1–12: When he returned to Capernaum after some days, it was reported that he was at home. So many gathered around that there was no longer room for them, not even in front of the door; and he was speaking the word to them. Then some people came, bringing to him a paralyzed man, carried by four of them. And when they could not bring him to Jesus because of the crowd, they removed the roof above him; and after having dug through it, they let down the mat on which the paralytic lay. When Jesus saw their

> faith, he said to the paralytic, "Son, your sins are forgiven." Now some of the scribes were sitting there, questioning in their hearts, "Why does this fellow speak in this way? It is blasphemy! Who can forgive sins but God alone?" At once Jesus perceived in his spirit that they were discussing these questions among themselves; and he said to them, "Why do you raise such questions in your hearts? Which is easier, to say to the paralytic, 'Your sins are forgiven,' or to say, 'Stand up and take your mat and walk'? But so that you may know that the Son of Man has authority on earth to forgive sins"—he said to the paralytic—"I say to you, stand up, take your mat and go to your home." And he stood up, and immediately took the mat and went out before all of them; so that they were all amazed and glorified God, saying, "We have never seen anything like this!"

When Jesus forgives a paralytic his sins, the scribes are perturbed and they discuss among themselves by saying that only God is able to do that. But Jesus guesses their thoughts and reacts by making the man walk. This time again, the kernel of the narrative is not the healing of the paralytic, but the discussion concerning the power that Jesus has exercised. In particular, it appears clearly from now on in fact that this is the picture of God that is in play. By the deeds and acts of Jesus, people in the story see themselves confronted with their picture of God. Whether God can forgive sins does not constitute a shocking opinion. But that Jesus can do the same thing? The reasoning of the scribes squares well with the form of questioning we have just rejected. They have their preconceived idea of a God according to whom it is unthinkable that a human being arrogates to himself the right to forgive sins. But here too it is appropriate to formulate the question in a different way: Who therefore is ready to consider Jesus' action as being part of a picture of God? And are those who have their own picture of God disposed to let it crumble to reconstruct something new from the existing fragments? The four bearers of the paralytic have total "faith." They dare to approach Jesus. It is characteristic of this meeting that neither the paralytic nor the bearers ask the slightest question. The power of Jesus is reinforced even more by the fact that it uniquely belongs to him. The evangelist moreover explicitly describes the surprise of the people at Jesus' powers. And nevertheless he boasts about it in no way but the result is that all glorify God.

The consequences of the forgiveness of sins are obviously not negligible. It is a sick man who is forgiven. Jesus makes the choice to reintegrate a man whom society had in some way banned. We would moreover have expected another succession of interventions: first healing, then forgiveness. But by choosing this order in the narrative, the author emphasizes the element of power in Jesus' identity. This is precisely the point that perturbs and shocks the scribes. It is not the healing that causes a problem, but the relationship between Jesus and God. And it is thus that throughout the narrative and the significance suggested by the evangelist, the reader is led little by little to reflect on Jesus' identity.

What is striking in the two narratives mentioned above is that Jesus himself neither confirms nor denies that he is a man of God. We will come back to this later, but it is in every way others who interpret his action as coming from God (the demon, the scribes, the spectators), while Jesus keeps his distance. On the contrary, the narrator's viewpoint is clear: he is obviously on the side of those who overflow with admiration and glorify God by saying of Jesus that they have never seen such a thing. His picture of God is indirectly expressed by others. Following these two pericopes implying questions, it is clear that in the eyes of the reader, certain positions in the gospel narrative are already taken. Jesus brings the Kingdom of God by acting in the sense of liberation and healing. His action provokes conflict with the scribes. The readers see themselves challenged to make a picture of God for themselves beginning with the way Jesus acts. The narrator gives valuable help to the readers by suggesting that Jesus is different from all other people.

More Questions and Criticism from His Enemies

The opponents of Jesus will come back several times in the Gospel to ply Jesus with questions. If the questions are critical, the intentions are obviously hostile. They, however, contribute to specifying the picture of Jesus that the narrator seeks to communicate, because these opponents represent a picture of God that does not correspond to that of Jesus. Perhaps the profoundest discussion at the level of content between Jesus and the scribes treats the fundamental inspiration that is at the base of Jesus' life. This debate comes relatively early in the Gospel. The scribes who came down from Jerusalem to Galilee accuse Jesus by saying:

> Mark 3:22 "He has Beelzebul, and by the ruler of the demons he casts out demons."

In other words, they accuse Jesus of being on the side of Satan (Beelzebul) and not on the side of God. For the readers, this criticism expresses the fundamental choice before which the behavior of Jesus places them. Does Jesus do good or evil? Thanks to the information furnished earlier in the Gospel, they are aware of the fact that Jesus conquered Satan in the desert and that he cast out demons. But now people appear who accuse him of being himself possessed by Satan. This encourages readers to reflection, because why do the official representatives of a religion judge Jesus in such a crushing way? What are their motives, what is their God?

Jesus replies to these criticisms in his turn by asking questions under the form of an enigma:

> Mark 3:23–26: And he called them to him, and spoke to them in parables, "How can Satan cast out Satan? If a kingdom is divided against itself, that kingdom cannot stand. And if a house is divided against itself, that house will not be able to stand. And if Satan has risen up against himself and is divided, he cannot stand, but his end has come.

This is a reply that can help readers in their reflection because it proposes elements to elaborate the picture of God. Jesus is convinced that what he does corresponds to God's will. And according to Jesus God is stronger than Satan for the reasons that he mentions right after. Jesus says that "people will be forgiven for their sins and whatever blasphemies they utter; but whoever blasphemes against the Holy Spirit can never have forgiveness, but is guilty of an eternal sin" (Mark 3:28–29). These are not easy words. We strike again against a language that forces readers to make a decision. To consciously claim that Jesus is motivated by satanic powers and not by the Spirit of God means that we put ourselves radically outside a relationship with God. This also means that Jesus is convinced that all other people can count on God.

As the narrator pushes the conflict with the opponents to the extreme, enormous differences clearly appear between the way the God of Jesus thinks and that of the official religious representatives about the same God. The story of the paralytic taught us that the first reproach the scribes made to Jesus concerns his "blasphemous" language. This discussion about blasphemy constitutes the beginning of the guiding thread that will diametrically contrast the two parties until the end of the Gospel. In the eyes of his adversaries, Jesus commits blasphemous acts. It is striking that at the end of the Gospel the decisive weight of the accusation brought to the trial of Jesus again still concerns this same charge of blasphemy.

And once Jesus is on the cross, Mark writes that the passers-by abused him by shaking their heads and mocking him. Here too we find the same root since literally it is written, "they blasphemed him" (Mark 15:29). This thematic arc between the beginning and the end of the Gospel lets us interpret everything that is relevant about the conflict between Jesus and his opponents in the light of the construction of a picture of God. Here again are a few of these critical questions to illustrate this proposal. If we can read them as the expression of a criticism of Jesus, they also indicate nevertheless what attitude Mark invites us to have about Jesus and God.

- When he is at table in the presence of Pharisees, the latter say, "Why does he eat with with tax collectors and sinners? (Mark 2:16).
- When the disciples of Jesus pluck some ears of wheat, they ask Jesus, "Look, why are they doing what is not lawful on the sabbath?" (Mark 2:24).
- The spectators also notice the difference between the group around Jesus and the others: "Why do John's disciples and the disciples of the Pharisees fast, but your disciples do not fast?" (Mark 2:18).
- In a reaction to a trap question, this time coming from the Sadducees concerning the resurrection, Jesus replies with another question, "Is not this the reason why you are wrong, that you know neither the scriptures nor the power of God?" And a bit further, "He is God not of the dead, but of the living; you are quite wrong" (Mark 12:24, 27).

Not to Generalize

Mark seeks to develop a conflict over different pictures of God. The characterization of the adversaries is made on the basis of the relationship between Jesus and God. It is therefore important to avoid every generalization tending to stick one or the other label on the adversaries. Jesus does not speak of another God. He believes in the same God as his Jewish entourage. Just as for the scribes, the Torah is for him an essential part in the understanding of what God wants and who God is. Without there being the slightest possible misunderstanding, the author demonstrates that Jesus uses the same beginning points as his adversaries to speak of God. Following a discussion between Jesus and the scribes, one of the latter approaches Jesus and asks him a question in the presence of other people:

> Mark 12:28–34: [. . .] "Which commandment is the first of all?" Jesus answered, "The first is: '*Hear, O Israel: the Lord our God, the Lord is one; you shall love the Lord your God with all your heart, and with all your soul, and with all your mind, and all your strength*'. *The second is this, 'You shall love your neighbor as yourself.'* There is no other commandment greater than these." Then the scribe said to him, "You are right, Teacher, you have truly said that '*he is one, and besides him there is no other*'; and '*to love him with all the heart, and with all the understanding, and with all the* strength,' and '*to love one's neighbor as oneself*,'—this is much more important than all whole burnt offerings and sacrifices." When Jesus saw that he answered wisely, he said to him, "You are not far from the kingdom of God." After that no one dared to ask him any question.

Let's observe first for a moment the style proper to the evangelist. It is indeed a matter of a discussion about the Scriptures and the scribe picks up almost word for word Jesus' reply. This doublet well shows that there is no fundamental divergence concerning "the first commandment." But it cannot escape readers that the meeting ends in a somewhat enigmatic way. Both Jesus' conclusion ("You are not far from the kingdom of God") and the scribes' reaction ("And no one dared to ask him any question") express on the one hand Jesus' authority, but on the other hand a hesitation to totally congratulate the man in question. If he has answered correctly, why does not Jesus say to him that he can enter the Kingdom of God? Why does he say explicitly that he is "not far" from the kingdom? We are here in front of an example of what we have previously called a "gap" in the narration, a lacuna to be filled in by the reader. Through the response of Jesus, readers are confronted with themselves and they perhaps risk having the same reaction as the scribes: silence. Readers probably hold in their heads that at the theoretic level Jesus and the scribe give an identical reply. Granted that there remain differences in the interpretation of this commandment and in the concrete way of putting it into practice. The fact that the scribe adds in his reply to Jesus that this double commandment means a lot more than "all offering and all sacrifice" is probably true, but it also betrays the thinking of this man. His thought remains still rooted in the ritual climate of sacrifice. For Jesus, it had absolutely nothing to do with that.

Beating of a Butterfly's Wings

We just described a simple literary phenomenon: people wonder who Jesus is. But as in chaos theory in which the simple beating of a butterfly's wings could be the catalyst of a tornado at the other end of the world, this simple questioning also runs the risk of involving confusion. The frequency of these questions moreover means that it is impossible that there can be any unconscious carelessness on the part of the author. It is an extremely well-reflected strategy, intended to give a dynamic to the narrative and with great consequences for the experience of the readers since it creates a tension in the story. By insisting so strongly on the questioning behavior of those who surround Jesus, the evangelist sees to it that the role of the protagonist becomes essential. The Gospel is "Jesus-centric." There are centripetal forces focused on Jesus. Everything and everyone turns around him. By comparing Mark with the more voluminous Gospels of Matthew and Luke, we see that precisely by its brevity the text of Mark focuses on the identity of Jesus. Up until now, we have stopped only for the questions of the adversaries of Jesus. But, in the text, all the questions asked—and whoever asks them—contribute to the formation of a picture of Jesus. We will speak again in chapter 7 of the conversations between Jesus and his disciples. But there are also the people of his own village who do not understand. When he goes back to his birthplace, we hear criticisms. It arises once again of these words that Jesus' teaching and acts must be considered as a unity (wisdom and miracles). But what is striking above all is that they ask explicit questions about his identity. Who are his brothers and sisters and mother?

> Mark 6:2–3: On the sabbath he began to teach in the synagogue, and many who heard him were astounded. They said, "Where did this man get all this? What is this wisdom that has been given to him? What deeds of power are being done by his hands! Is not this the carpenter, the son of Mary and brother of James and Joses and Judas and Simon, and are not his sisters here with us?" And they took offense at him.

We have said and repeated that such questions are intended to make readers reflect about Jesus' identity. And at the heart of this question lies the relationship between Jesus and God. Each time, the questions suggest that what concerns Jesus is at root more than the humanly possible. However, the evangelist is not satisfied to ask questions about Jesus. Sometimes he also gives answers. But readers should know that they do not always have to seek these answers in the same place where they find the questions. There too we have an example of the way we expect the readers to approach the text with a large dose of creativity. They should also establish a connection between the above passage and an earlier discussion about the relationship between Jesus, his family, and God. At a given moment, Jesus' family seeks for him because they are of the opinion that he "has lost his senses." Having been informed by the people who surround him that his mother, his brothers, and sisters are looking for him, he replies:

> Mark 3:33–35: "Who are my mother and my brothers?" And looking at those who surround him, he said, "Here are my mother and my brothers! Whoever does the will of God is my brother and sister and mother."

It is in these verses that we in fact find a reply to the questioning of the people of Jesus' village. The readers at the same time recall that, for Jesus, it is in no way a confirmation of one's own position. The most important thing is that God's will is done. We will speak again of this criterion in the chapter on the disciples.

But What Is a Gospel?

We are not surprised by it today, but Mark's initiative of writing the first narrative about Jesus was for his time a perfectly innovative act in literature. As to literary genre, the Gospel is absolutely new. Scholarship has examined whether it was possible to identify this new genre with one of the current literary forms at this time, but every time we have been confronted with too many differences. We could envisage different genres, but the Gospel is not a Greek drama; not a biography as it exists for other divine men; not a "life" of an emperor; not a tragedy; not a philosophical treatise between a master and his disciples. The Gospel is singular in this that it mentions the memory of the person Jesus, not only to provide information about him but also to create an existential link with him. The evangelist has in his literary luggage the questions of his time that he inserts into his descriptions of Jesus as he was. This description is therefore a reflection of the way in which Jesus was experienced in the narrator's time. And as it was a narrative of the past in the present, the genre became unique and very powerful. Be that as it may, the questions in the Gospel are intended to insist on the central role of Jesus. As a consequence, the first thing that readers do in reading Mark is to ask themselves questions. The Gospel does not present itself as a book filled with immovable certitudes, but rather as inspired by a groping interest. It is important not to neglect this background when we seek in the Gospel expressions or positive definitions of Jesus. The questioning is a necessary attraction to an eventual relationship between readers and the main character, Jesus. By imagining that they are in the skin of a questioning opponent, readers are confronted with a first decision: Is Jesus on the side of good or evil? The reply contains the first key to the code allowing us to open the text. If someone already disconnects here, he will no longer be able to see himself questioning in what follows.

It can seem audacious even for a second to envisage that Jesus can find himself on the side of evil. But to place him there is perfectly realistic when we are conscious of the consequences of the conflict between Jesus and the authorities. It is, among other things, the critical and negative attitude of the authorities that led to Jesus' death. The rejection of Jesus can take such dimensions that we prefer at the end to see him dead rather than alive. If we were writing the story of Jesus from the viewpoint of his adversaries, it would not be a "gospel" at all. Jesus appears to them as a threat, above all by the great part of liberty that Jesus is authorized to take in the exercise of his authority. We saw above that he acts with authority and that his deeds and actions provoke a conflict over power. He proves threatening for the established hierarchy because he has a different view of the world, people, and God. But this will not be a fight on equal footing. The dominant authorities, who not only represent political and military but also religious power, plot to destroy him. Jesus is a solitary innovator who, moreover makes no call to violence and does not gather his disciples around him as an armed troop. The narrator, too, has taken his place in this combat. He will be on the side of the solitary Jesus. And this choice can be explained only in one way: he is convinced that Jesus is finally closer to God than his adversaries. In order that his readers can better judge what exactly are the challenges they will face they must also learn to know the relationship of the other actors in the story to Jesus.

Once Again: Reading in Reality

We explained at the beginning of this chapter that all interpretation of the Gospel begins with the real reader. We applied this principle to the questions posed by the adversaries to discover that the aim of these questions is to confront readers with a choice. The mechanism functions so that readers pick up for themselves the questions of the adversaries and then seek to find an answer. Mark invented the "gospel" genre as an artistic form so he could stir up a dialogue between Jesus and the real readers of Mark's time. But the narrative reading reveals to us that this dialogue continues to pursue new real readers.

In the debates, there are not only the adversaries to ask questions. The narrator equally puts some in Jesus' mouth. What is striking is that Jesus himself replies to most of the questions he asks. This gives readers a better idea of Jesus' thinking. By giving the answers himself, Jesus appears to be more clever than his opponents. Even more so because the opponents remain silent. Here are a few examples:

> Mark 2:19: Jesus said to them, "The wedding guests cannot fast while the bridegroom is with them, can they? As long as they have the bridegroom with them, they cannot fast. [. . .]" [Notice again the doublet!]

> Mark 2:25–26: And he said to them, "Have you never read what David did when he and his companions were hungry and in need of food? He entered the house of God, when Abiathar was high priest, and ate the bread of the Presence, which it is not lawful for any but the priests to eat, and he gave some to his companions."

> Mark 3:4–5: Then he said to them, "Is it lawful to do good or to do harm on the Sabbath, to save life or to kill?" But they were silent. He looked around to them with anger; he was grieved at their hardness of heart and said to the man, "Stretch out your hand."

> Mark 8:12–13: And he sighed deeply in his spirit and said, "Why does this generation ask for a sign? Truly I tell you, no sign will be given to this generation." And he left them, and getting into the boat again, he went across to the other side.

And when the opponents try nevertheless to respond, they do not know what to say.

> Mark 11:29–33: Jesus said to them, "I will ask you one question; answer me, and I will tell you by what authority I do these things. Did the baptism of John come from heaven, or was it of human

> origin? Answer me." [. . .] So they answered Jesus, "We do not know."

For the majority of these questions and answers, it is not possible to transpose them directly to the time of modern readers. The discussions are much too implicated in their culture and their time. The original Jewish readers would more easily place them and they would find textual indications to understand how Jesus was concretely different. To grasp clearly the "point" of each of these discussions, contemporary readers need a sum of information about the laws and customs of that time. That is not part of our subject and objective here. But even for contemporary readers, these discussions show that Jesus did not want to break radically with the living traditions and that, on the contrary, he had on essential points divergent ideas from those of the most important religious leaders of his time. We could not ignore this critical and prophetic attitude of the picture of Jesus such as it is proposed to us by Mark.

However, a single question of Jesus rises above the centuries and keeps, by its universality, all its pertinence for the real readers of every time. This remarkable question is perhaps also the best known, "But for you, who am I?" (Mark 8:29). The question is not addressed to his adversaries but to his disciples; it seems therefore to be more a part of the intimate sphere of the personal relationships with Jesus than of theological debate. The adversaries are too far away to be able to answer such a question. It is a question that invites us to give a personal answer. The question does not so much accentuate Jesus' identity but much more what the disciples think of him. And this time, in all logic but contrary to the other questions, he does not give an answer. Chapter 7 will go into more depth about what the relationship between Jesus and the disciples can mean for real readers. It is a personal question that Jesus addresses to his disciples and through them to each of the real readers.

For Further Reading

Dormeyer, D. *Das Markusevangelium als Idealbiographie von Jesus Christus, dem Nazarener.* Stuttgarter Biblische Beiträge 43. Stuttgart: Katholisches Bibelwerk, 1999.

Harrington, W. J. *Mark, Realistic Theologian: The Jesus of Mark.* 2nd ed. Dublin: Columba, 2000.

Kingsbury, J. D. *The Christology of Mark's Gospel.* Philadelphia: Fortress, 1983.

Matera, F. J. *What Are They Saying about Mark?* New York: Paulist, 1987 (see esp. pp. 18–37).

McInerny, W. F., "An Unresolved Question in the Gospel Called Mark: 'Who Is This Whom Even Wind and Sea Obey?' (4:41)" *Perspectives in Religious Studies* 23 (1996) 255–68.

Müller, P. *"Wer ist dieser?" Jesus im Markusevangelium: Markus als Erzähler, Verkündiger und Lehrer.* Biblisch-theologische Studien. Neukirchen: Neukirchener, 1995.

Naluparayil, J. C. "Jesus of the Gospel of Mark: Present State of Research." *Currents in Research: Biblical Studies* 8 (2000) 191–226.

———. *The Identity of Jesus in Mark: Essay on Narrative Christology.* Studium Biblicum Franciscanum. Analecta 49. Jerusalem: Franciscan, 2000.

Tannehill, R. C. "The Gospel of Mark as Narrative Christology." *Semeia* 16 (1980) 57–95.

6

The Burden of Honorary Titles

Introduction

All these questions about Jesus teach readers that it is not obvious at all to end up circumventing the identity of the person. In addition, the somewhat vague use of the honorific titles conceded to Jesus constitute another aspect of the content explained by Mark's way of telling. There again, it is a surprising narrative element for contemporary readers. They are indeed numerous who associate Jesus with "Son of God." It is an obvious association, often based on tradition without the slightest hesitation. Ever since then, believers are those who fully mark their agreement with the creed: "I believe in one Lord, Jesus Christ, the only Son of God," whereas unbelievers are those who reject this creed: for them, Jesus was a being of exceptional goodness, but there have been others like him. The two groups thus find themselves in opposition. Now the narrator of the Gospel of Mark broaches the question in quite a different way. He does not describe in black and white categories, in which one would treat Jesus with the titles that he must have or not have. The contrast is not located at the level of those who believe and those who do not believe (especially not when the only stake is a question of profession of correct faith). It seems likely that in Mark's text, the narrator goes beyond this polemic. This interpretation moreover agrees completely with what I was able to write in the introduction, that is, this Gospel is intended for everyone. It is not necessary to have previously established whether one is a believer or not to find a meaning in this text. It would be a false alternative in relation to Mark's Gospel. Faith does not depend first of all on a correct profession of faith. It must find its place in the process of growth in the life of every human being, with as a principal element the encounter with Jesus. The evangelist is convinced that a meeting with Jesus has consequences for the way to grapple with life. Without wishing to depart completely from the original context, a *narrative* Christology thus seems to be the most likely way to reflect on the identity of Jesus. It begins in fact with the dynamic of the narrative and not with historical or philological analysis of titles. When the question of titles is raised later, it will be in relation with their function in the narrative. Where do we find them? How often? Who makes use of them and who does not? Do they produce a conflict? Or are they on the contrary approved?

Jesus and His Honorary Titles

In scholarship on Mark's Gospel, one of the great subjects of debate is which title best expresses the opinion of the evangelist about Jesus. These names of Jesus are called "christological titles" because they designate the lordship or the divinity of Jesus. These titles indeed contain the belief of the first Christians and for this reason they are important. They reveal when and in what groups we can start to speak of Jesus in such and such a way. From what concerns Mark, it is concretely "Son of God," "Messiah," or "Christ," "Son of man," "Son of David," and "Lord." It does not seem very difficult to verify which of these titles corresponds best to Mark's own view. We can indeed very reasonably admit that the title mentioned in the heading of his work—it is thus that we can consider the first verse—expresses his personal opinion.

> Mark 1:1: The beginning of the good news of Jesus Christ, the Son of God.

According to the narrator, Jesus is the Son of God and Christ. I have to observe for concern with honesty that scholars continue to discuss whether the words "Son of God" were actually part of the original text. We cannot exclude the possibility that they were added later. But on the basis of the internal arguments that reinforce the narrative cohesion, we can reasonably suspect that "Son of God" could have been part of the first verse. And whatever the case may be, if we seek to explain the significance of this verse, we will have to, broadly speaking, comment on each of the words used. At least the words "gospel," "Christ," and "Son of God" already have quite a history before Mark used them. It is therefore appropriate to ask about how these titles were understood in the light of their pre-history. The meaning of these titles is one of the examples that have been mentioned in the introduction on the linguistic and cultural abyss that separates the past and the present. We will only be able to understand these terms when we have an idea of their meaning in the past. That's why I propose a survey of the most important titles with a commentary.

However, it is not sufficient to know the background of a title to understand the message of the evangelist. At best we have then understood what are the sources of inspiration and the tradition of the author, but not at all how, in approaching this tradition in a creative way, he has been able to integrate it into his narrative. From the readers' viewpoint, it is especially important to be attentive to what happens to the existing titles in this totally new collection of the Gospel. We must, for example, take into account how the narrator uses titles with a lot of hesitation and "parsimony."

Son of God

"Son of God" does not appear very often in the Gospel, but it is obviously the term that the evangelist uses in the opening of his book. Here's the listing of the other occurrences.

Jesus is recognized as Son by a voice coming from heaven. Completely faithful to his style, Mark has us hear it twice in almost identical terms. At Jesus' baptism we hear:

> Mark 1:11: "You are my Son, the Beloved; with you I am well pleased".

And at the time of the meeting between Jesus and his disciples on the mountain, we read:

> Mark 9:7: "This is my Son, the Beloved; listen to him".

These two events in which God confirms that Jesus is his Son, agree with the thought of the evangelist about Jesus (1:1). From the narrative viewpoint, God and the evangelist have a common vision about Jesus. Then, the demons that have taken possession of the mind of some people also address Jesus as "Son of God." We mentioned above the first meeting of Jesus in the synagogue. We can quote others:

> Mark 3:11–12: Whenever the unclean spirits saw him, they fell down before him and shouted, "You are the Son of God!" But he sternly ordered them not to make him known.

> Mark 5:7: "What have you to do with me, Jesus, Son of the Most High God?"

> Compare with Mark 1:34: [. . .] and he cast out many demons; and he would not permit the demons to speak, because they knew him.

When Jesus is questioned by the high priest, the latter asks in his turn if he is the "Son of the Blessed One." This is an expression that is considered in general as a Jewish turn of phrase for "Son of God." We moreover find, just as in Mark 1:1, the combination of this expression with the term "Messiah." Jesus answers: "I am."

> Mark 14:61–62: But he was silent and did not answer. Again the high priest asked, "Are you the Messiah, the Son of the Blessed One?" Jesus said, "I am; and '*you will see the Son of man seated at the right hand of Power,*' and '*coming with the clouds of heaven.*'"

Finally, there are the famous words of the centurion at the foot of the cross who says at the moment of the death of Jesus:

> Mark 15:39: "Truly this man was God's Son!"

At first sight there cannot be a misunderstanding. Jesus is the Son of God. However, in attentively analyzing the passages concerned and placing them in their context, we notice that, apart from the first verse, there exists in the head of the narrator like a strange hesitation to be fully involved with this term. It would rather seem that the evangelist retains and does not strongly affirm Jesus' identity by means of this honorary title. Attentive readers will decipher several indications that reveal that, in his communication with readers, the author consciously uses this process.

Son of God and the Dynamic of Reading

In this paragraph I wish to deepen the narrative function of the references to the title "Son of God." If its use in the opening verse of the Gospel consists of information furnished to the readers, this same information remains hidden from the persons who appear in the narrative (the disciples,

Jesus' family, the adversaries) as the work proceeds. Only the readers are aware of this opinion of Mark that is not heard by any other of the people in the narrative. The latter moreover do not attain this profession of faith for themselves at any time, nor do they address Jesus in any positive way as Son of God. This creates the impression that during his lifetime Jesus cannot be recognized or addressed as Son of God. The narrator moreover reinforces this sentiment for the readers. Apparently, only the demons are capable of having this revelation concerning Jesus. Now, most of the time, they are summoned to be quiet (Mark 1:25, 32; 3:12). But it is not so surprising that the demons recognize Jesus. Aren't they part of the transcendental universe and isn't it logical as a result that they know what is happening? We know demons primarily through the apocryphal literature. Thus the demons in the apocryphal text *The Testament of Solomon* have specific foreknowledge. Ornias, one of those demons, explains this knowledge as follows: "We demons go up to the firmament of the heavens and we fly among the stars. And we hear the judgments concerning the souls of human beings." As for Mark, it remains strange that he seems very consciously to want to give his readers the sentiment that Jesus does not wish to be recognized as Son of God during his lifetime. Elizabeth Struthers Malbon speaks in this respect of a "deflected Christology." Jesus in fact takes great effort to reorient honor or respect for God.[1]

The question of the high priest at the time of the questioning of Jesus cannot be understood as a profession of faith in Jesus. He asks him if he is the Son of the Blessed One, which is the Jewish expression for Son of God (Mark 14:61). With what we know about the use of doublets in the text of Mark, we could have expected Jesus to repeat these terms. Now, he does not do it. He is content to say "I am" and in this way the terms "Messiah" and "Son of God" are relativized. In what follows in his reply is no explanation of the title "Son of God," but a description of the role to be filled by the *Son of man*. In this sense, it is completely suitable that the only human being who calls Jesus "Son of God" does so at the foot of the cross, at the moment of Jesus' death (Mark 15:39). The opinions of exegetes on the interpretation of the words of the centurion are rather diverse. They in general consider that it is a profession of Christian faith: the centurion is then the example par excellence of the pagan who is converted in recognizing Jesus as his God. But is that really the case? The words could equally be understood as

1. E. Struthers Malbon, *Mark's Jesus: Characterization as Narrative Christology*. Waco: Baylor University Press, 2009.

the expression of surprise on the part of a pagan soldier when he sees the extraordinary signs that surround Jesus' death. We must then understand, "He must be the son of a god." Unless he is uttering a remark filled with irony or derision, in the sense of "Ha ha! Here he is therefore, the Son of God! What a pretty place he occupies there." Other soldiers had preceded him on this path. What's clear is that there is no one in the narrative to receive this profession or this declaration. No one . . . except the readers. It was the same at the opening of the Gospel in which there was no one to hear the expression "Son of God." The readers are then left alone when they have heard the complete story about Jesus. At the time of Jesus' death, the disciples are eclipsed in the shadows.

One thing seems from now on very clear: Mark wants his readers to recognize Jesus as Son of God, but they can do it in a correct way only under certain conditions. And if these are lacking, the adequate use of this title appears difficult. In face of the fact that no human character recognizes Jesus as Son of God, we must say that the only one who without ambiguity names Jesus "Son" is God himself (Mark 1:9; 9:7; cf. 12:1–12). This contrasting effect accentuates even more the reservations uttered by Jesus with regard to the fact of being called "Son of God" by living persons. There is thus not only the fact that not a single human being recognizes Jesus; it is moreover explicitly declared that God clearly recognizes Jesus. And Jesus does not protest. From the narrative viewpoint, Mark writes so that each time God designates Jesus as his Son, no one else reacts: neither the first time with the Baptist, because this moment is presented as a private moment between God and Jesus (Mark 1:9), nor the second time on the mountain (Mark 9:7), because Jesus asks the three disciples present to be silent until after the resurrection. It therefore seems to me at the level of the reading process difficult to underestimate the importance of this prudence about the title "Son of God." If Jesus avoids for himself being called "Son of God," that can only be a warning to readers not to lightly declare that he is indeed "Son of God."

Son of God: The Hellenistic Context

I presume that one of the explanations of Mark's circumspection concerning the title "Son of God" is found in the fact that this expression was not unknown by his hearers. In fact, the evangelist has a problem. He seeks to tell something new about Jesus, but at the same time he has to call on existing expressions that his hearers have to recognize to some extent. How can he transmit something new about Jesus, Son of God, to hearers who know well this expression and who therefore have certain expectations about the content of it. This kind of expectation has been expressed in two articles by Adela Yarbro Collins.[2] This author contrasts the universes of Jewish and Hellenistic-Roman thought in the first century. Her starting point is developed in a way parallel to our own objective: How is the narrative received by readers? Her research confirms that the meaning of a text must never make an abstraction of the context of the real readers. However, she takes into account only the first real readers.

Let's take someone born and formed in a Hellenistic culture. In reading the different passages about Jesus, Son of God, they will give to them unquestionably their own interpretations. Jesus' baptism (Mark 1:9–11) will remind them that numerous wise men, politicians, or artists have received their inspiration from God. Or when they learn that Jesus heals people, they will recall the great tradition of many miracle workers that allocated to themselves a (quasi-)divine status and have been honored as such. The best known is Asclepius, of whom it is said that he healed the blind, made paralytics walk, and even raised one dead person. Moreover, in hearing Jesus called "Most High" (Mark 5:7) a good number could think of Zeus, who was celebrated by this title in several Mediterranean regions. The anecdote about Jesus who appears on the mountain all dressed in white (Mark 9:3) creates among non-Jews the connotation of divinities disguising themselves to go to the earth among humans. And that Jesus then imposes silence on his disciples (Mark 9:9) is easily understood as part of a strategy to not be recognized. The gift of prophecy equally carries a divine connotation among many contemporaries. Finally, we should not forget there are probably many of them that the name "Son of God" would have automatically made them think of the emperor. There exist from the first century piles of inscriptions, texts, or coins that witness to the divine status of the emperor.

We can ask if the ideas about the divine characteristics of Jesus that are formed at the beginning of the twenty-first century would be very different from those in vogue among the Romans and Hellenists of the first century. There are still many people today who style Jesus divine because he would

2. A. Yarbro Collins, "Mark and His Readers: The Son of God among Jews," *Harvard Theological Review* 92 (1999) 393–408; "Mark and His Readers: The Son of God among Greeks and Romans," *Harvard Theological Review* 93 (2000) 85–100.

have done things that would not set with generally admitted natural laws, or since he uses paranormal gifts, or would have done "extraordinary" acts. But the whole question is to know if such is the picture that the evangelist wanted to transmit of Jesus as Son of God. Is he perhaps giving a totally other significance to this divine status of Jesus?

Son of God: Canvas of the Jewish Background

From their side, readers of the Jewish tradition have been able to associate the expression "Son of God" with a huge series of texts. It involves a universe of thought with other representations of God. Even if the first century saw an important mixture or even a fusion of Greek and Jewish philosophical cultures, we easily imagine that the Jews understood the stories about Jesus and about his relations with God in a completely different way from their Greek or Roman contemporaries. Those familiar with the Old Testament would clearly see that the evangelist was referring in an explicit or implicit way to ancient texts. The story of Jesus' baptism (Mark 1:9–11), for example, recalls Psalm 2: "I will announce the decree of Yahweh. He said to me, 'You, my son, today I have given birth to you'" (Ps 2:7). God names the king of Israel his son. Or let's think of Isaiah, "Here is my servant that I uphold, my chosen one in whom my soul is pleased" (Isa 42:1). The royal ideology implies that the king is presented as a God, "Your throne, God [= the king] is for ever and ever, the scepter of your kingdom is a scepter of justice. You love justice, you hate crime. Thus God, your God, has given you the anointing with joy as none of your rivals" (Ps 45:7–8). A Jewish ear would not really be surprised that human beings are called sons or children of God. Not only individuals, but the whole people receive the epithet "Child of God." Known texts on this subject are: "Then you will say to Pharaoh, 'Thus said Yahweh: My first born son is Israel. I had told you, "Let my son go, so that he may serve me." Since you refuse to let him go, I am going to kill your first-born sons'" (Exod 4:22–23). "Yahweh your God, who walks ahead of you, will fight for you, just as you saw him do in Egypt. You saw him also in the desert. Yahweh your God upholds you as a man upholds his son, all along the route that you have followed until now" (Deut 1:30–31). We read again in the book of Wisdom that the opponents of just persons rebuke them for pretending that God is their father: "They flatter themselves to having known God and call themselves children of God [. . .] They say that happy is the final fate of just persons and they pride themselves to having God as father" (Wis 2:13–16). It is not impossible either that, at the time of Jesus, all pious Jews considered themselves children of God. In Ecclesiastes we find the prayers "Lord, father and master of my life" and "Lord, father and God of my life" (23:1–4).

By the title "Son of God," Jesus can be considered by the Jews as a royal descendant in the line of God and as a pious and just man. By the pouring out of the Holy Spirit at the time of his baptism, he could have been equally seen as a person with prophetic gifts (cf. the prophet in Isa 61). But some Jews will certainly have been astonished to read in Mark an identification of the Son of God with the figure of the Messiah. This identification signifies in effect that, as well as being Son of God, Jesus was equally the Christ (the anointed one) whom they were expecting to free Israel. Other Jews held this ultimate identification between the two as perfectly plausible. Especially if they resorted to certain texts of the Qumran community, because we find there the expectation that a Messiah who descended from the house of David would come, who would equally be called Son of God and who would restore a kingdom of peace.

Why Is Jesus So Specific?

We could conclude from what precedes that, in the milieu in which the Gospel of Mark circulated, they were not too much surprised by this appellation "Son of God." But this statement throws the ball to the readers: Why does the evangelist take so much precaution about this title? As for me, I see two plausible explanations. First—and this completes what has been said earlier—Mark's preferred title reveals its deepest significance only at the end of a long process. In doing so, the narrator encourages the readers to consider the identity of Jesus for themselves as they read the Gospel and abandon all preconceived ideas. By leaving behind a pre-established conception of God, we are inevitably confronted by a criticism from the narrator. The meaning of reading is not to seek confirmation of what we know or believe already. It is rather the opposite: in the course of their reading, readers can seek to know if it is possible to give a title to Jesus and if so, what one. These titles make sense through or throughout the life of Jesus as Mark tells it. That's why Mark renounces a correct profession of faith about Jesus during his lifetime and that's still why silence is imposed on the demons. The importance of the titles is in fact secondary, because even without the correct title, an encounter with Jesus is possible. Is it that the one who proclaims Jesus as Son of God is at a higher level than those who do not? That remains completely fuzzy. It would seem that the erroneous use of titles for Jesus is a more serious fault than not to use these titles at all.

Second, the hesitation that Jesus proves with regard to his identification by others as far as Son of God is concerned means that attention is not turned away from his existence as a human being. By insisting too much on his divine aspect, we risk too easily no longer considering him as the human being Jesus, originating in Nazareth. Now Mark wishes readers to be surprised that this concrete person is at the same time Son of God. Therefore, let us leave Jesus a human being. Here again, we appeal to readers: there must be in the story of this person something exceptional and contradictory in comparison with all human expectations. If Jesus was only called Son of God, there is every chance that we would not admit any longer that he was "one of us," which Mark seeks to avoid at all costs. It is essential that Jesus be human among humans. If we are eager to allude to a "secret" in this Gospel, this is it: that the evangelist wants to know nothing about all profession of faith that would affirm anything that would be a detriment to the humanity of Jesus. This "secret" also explains why Mark only lets God alone legitimately call Jesus Son of God, as if the evangelist wanted to help his readers to understand that Jesus can only be called Son of God by people once these same people have accepted that God calls him his Son.

All this is part of the very essence of the narrative. The evangelist expresses at the narrative level what his theology, his conception of God, and of the relations of God with Jesus are. This relationship between God and Jesus is unique because God considers the human Jesus as unique and not because people consider Jesus as someone so fantastic that they push him away, so to speak, into the heavens. There is not a single compelling proof in the actions and words of Jesus that makes him so absolutely different or exceptional that people would have to consider him as divine. In Mark's idea, to encumber Jesus with the title "Son of God" does not come from the discovery of one or another quality of Jesus that would make him superior to anyone else and through which we would be conscious of his power. As for readers, we can only call him thus after having gone straight into the narrative, after having been "drubbed" by his life to arrive at the statement that this life is worth taking seriously. And the narrative bears a guarantee that God as father is on the side of Jesus. The narrative about Jesus is indeed as human as that. Such was the human being Jesus.

The Christ

Other than "Son of God," the appellation "Christ" has without a doubt the highest christological tenor. The Greek word "Christos" is a synonym for "Messiah" or "anointed one." Although it appears seven times in the course of this Gospel, this title "Christ" has a relevance for Christology only three times. We have already mentioned two of them: the opening of the Gospel (Mark 1:1) and the interrogation by the high priest (Mark 14:61). The third is found in Peter's reply to this basic question of Jesus, "But for you, who am I?" (We will come back to this passage when we mention the disciples and Jesus.) We generally designate this passage as Peter's profession of faith:

> Mark 8:27–30: Jesus went on with his disciples to the villages of Caesarea Philippi; and on the way he asked his disciples, "Who do people say that I am?" And they answered him, "John the Baptist; and others, Elijah; and still others, one of the prophets." He asked them, "But who do you say that I am?" Peter answered him, "You are the Messiah." And he sternly ordered them not to tell anyone about him.

In Peter's reply, the evangelist thus returns to "Christ" in the first verse of his text. This is the first time since the heading that the name "Christ" appears and it is the first time that Jesus' disciples recognize him positively. But as Christopher Tuckett rightly observes, we can ask ourselves about the weight the term "Christ" can have in Mark.[3] It is indeed striking that after Peter's profession of faith as well as after the question of the high priest, Jesus' reaction is full of criticism or at least nuance. Each time his reply contains a reference to another title, "Son of man." To contemporary readers used to pronouncing the expression "Jesus Christ" together, it can seem a bit bizarre that the earliest evangelist rarely refers to Jesus as the Christ and that the few times he does, he hastens to correct by a reference to the Son of man.

The Other Titles

Scholars agree universally that in Mark two titles have only a small significance: "Lord" and "Son of David." But "Son of man" draws our attention, only because it appears fourteen times or more and is only expressed by

3. C. M. Tuckett, *Christology and the New Testament: Jesus and His Earliest Followers* (Louisville: Westminster John Knox, 2001) 110–12.

Jesus. We have noticed for a long time that the expression is tied to two semantic fields. First, Jesus uses this term when he alludes to the Passion, the suffering that awaits him. The announcements of the Passion comprise a typical example, but there are also other passages. The second context occurs in eschatological mythic language. The Son of man is then the one who will be established by God after his Passion and will come to judge after his return to earth. He will have the power over history because God confers it on him. The evangelist has begun to interpret the Scriptures, in particular the vision in Daniel 7, and he applies it to Jesus.

> Mark 8:38: Those who are ashamed of me and of my words in this adulterous and sinful generation, of them the Son of man will also be ashamed when he comes in the glory of his Father with the holy angels.

> Mark 13:26–27: Then they will see "the Son of man coming in clouds" with great power and glory. Then he will send the angels, and gather his elect from the four winds, from the ends of the earth to the ends of heaven.

> Mark 14:61–62: But he was silent and did not answer. Again the high priest asked, "Are you the Messiah, the Son of the Blessed One?" Jesus said, "I am; and '*you will see the Son of man seated at the right hand of Power*,' and '*coming with the clouds of heaven*.'"

The characteristics attached to the title "Son of man" point the way to readers so that they will discover some basic content concerning Mark's vision of Jesus. Except in Mark 2:10 and 2:28, in which "son of man" signifies quite simply "man," the expression is found exclusively in the second part of the Gospel, that is to say, where the Passion occupies the preponderant place (Mark 8:31; 9:9, 12, 31; 10:33, 45; 14:21, 41). Since Jesus is the only one to use it, we could not claim that it is a christological title in the strict sense. The Gospel does not indicate the slightest tendency to push readers to make a profession of faith to Jesus as Son of man. Jesus does not ask that we recognize him as Son of man and the evangelist does not mention it in the opening of his text. In addition, God does not address his Son as Son of man. But the term keeps all its relevance for readers. They indeed understand how Mark makes Jesus speak of himself through a paradox: he is the suffering servant and he possesses at the same time the power that allows him to judge the world. This leads us to an important element that enlightens the way in which readers compose an opinion of Jesus. If readers want to recognize Jesus as Son of God, they will have to involve the perspective of Jesus about himself. This perspective is ambivalent: Jesus will suffer but he will be restored by God.

We said above that power is the stake of conflict between Jesus and his opponents. Beginning with Jesus' own perception, in which suffering and glorification by God occupy a central place, the two references to the Son of man in the first part of the Gospel have a deep significance. Twice Jesus takes part in a dispute with the opponents:

> Mark 2:10: But so that you may know that the Son of Man has authority on earth to forgive sins, [. . .].

> Mark 2:27–28: "The sabbath was made for humankind, and not humankind for the sabbath; so the Son of Man is lord even of the sabbath."

In intervening with authority and giving freely his own interpretation of the traditional picture of God and the equally traditional application of the laws, Jesus makes reference to what awaits him: the Passion. By using the title Son of man in Galilee, he forecasts the fate of the Son of man in Jerusalem. Thus, the evangelist is in a position to proclaim only a little later, after the first conflicts with the opponents:

> Mark 3:6: The Pharisees went out and immediately conspired with the Herodians against him, how to destroy him.

The Secret

The evangelist recounts that only God finally recognizes Jesus in his true identity. For us human beings there will always remain something inexplicable and very specific about this figure of Jesus. But what therefore is inexplicable about Jesus? What makes him different? If there is nothing objectively measurable, nothing that can prove by way of support, how can we find the trace of a key that would give access to the secret? To answer this question, we must hollow out another narrative line of this story: that of the relationship between Jesus and his disciples. Unlike the adversaries, they are those who are nearest Jesus. They hear the heart of his message. The dynamic emerging from this relationship leads readers to the dimension of the narrative that has been unexplored so far in this book: the suffering of Jesus, the Passion.

We have discovered at the beginning of the chapter about the questions relating to Jesus that a kind of centripetal force is created. Readers see themselves drawn to Jesus. The titles provoke an analogous effect. They install a person on a pedestal and stir up feelings of attraction and admiration. But as Mark creates the portrait of a Jesus to whom he is reluctant to attribute titles, there is born in this Gospel at the same time a centrifugal force. Readers seem themselves repulsed by the divine dimension of Jesus. The message of the evangelist is: if Jesus is the Son of God, know that he is very much also a human like us. The narrative line that we will now cross must hollow out even more this human being, Jesus. The evangelist does not affirm only that Jesus is a human being; he also says he is a suffering human being. And this is not a little thing to ask readers to understand.

For Further Reading

Baarlink. H. *Bist du der Christus, der Sohn des Hochgelobtes? Implizite und explizite Christologie im Markusevangelium*. Kamper Cahiers 74. Kampen: KOK, 1992.

Boring, M. E. "The Christology of Mark: Hermeneutical Issues for Systematic Theology." *Semeia* 30 (1984) 125–53.

———. "Markan Christology: God-Language for Jesus?" *New Testament Studies* 45 (1999) 451–71.

Broadhead, E. K. *Naming Jesus: Titular Christology in the Gospel of Mark*. JSNTSupp 175. Sheffield: University Press, 1999.

Cook, M. L. *Christology as Narrative Quest*. Collegeville, MN: Liturgical, 1997. (See esp. "A Biblical Image: 'The Beloved Son' in the Gospel of Mark," pp. 67–108).

Davis, P. G. "Mark's Christological Paradox." *Journal for the Study of the New Testament* 35 (1989) 3–18.

Fuller, R., and P. Perkins. *Who Is This Christ? Gospel Christology and Contemporary Faith*. Philadelphia: Fortress, 1983 ("Mark as Narrative Christology," 67–80).

Klauck, H.-J. *Vorspiel im Himmel: Erzähltecknik und Theologie im Markusprolog*. Biblisch-theologische Studien 32. Neukirchen: Neukirchener, 1997.

Kmiecik, U. *Der Menschensohn im Markusevangelium*. Forschung zur Bible 81. Wurzburg: Echter, 1997.

Müller, U. B. "'Sohn Gottes'—messianischer Hoheitstitel Jesu." *Zeitschrift für die neutestsamentliche Wissenschaft* 87 (1996) 1–32.

Sabin, M. N. *Reopening the Word: Reading Mark as Theology in the Context of Early Judaism*. Oxford: University Press, 2002.

Scholtissek, K. "'Er ist nicht ein Gott der Toten, sondern der Lebenden' (Mk 12,27): Grundzüge der markinischen Theologie." In *Der lebendige Gott: Beiträge zur Theologie des Neuen Testaments*, edited by T. Söding, 71–100. Festschrift Wilhelm Thüsing. Neutestamentliche Abhandlungen NT 31. Münster: Aschendorff, 1996.

———. "Der Sohn Gottes für das Reich Gottes. Zur Verbindung von Christologie und Eschatologie bei Markus." In *Der Evangelist als Theologe: Studien zum Markusevangelium*, edited by T. Söding, 63–90. Stuttgarter Bibelstudien 163. Stuttgart: Katholisches Bibelwerk, 1995.

Struthers Malbon, E. "The Christology of Mark's Gospel: Narrative Christology and the Markan Jesus." In *Who Do You Say I Am? Essays on Christology*, edited by M. A. Powell and D. R. Bauer, 33–48. Festschrift J. D. Kingsbury. Louisville: Westminster John Knox, 1999 (on the Christology that is rejected).

———. *Mark's Jesus: Characterization as Narrative Christology.* Waco: Baylor University Press, 2009.

Theobald, M. "Gottessohn und Menschensohn: Zur polaren Struktur der Christologie im Markusevangelium." *Studien zum Neuen Testament und seiner Umwelt* 13 (1988) 37–79.

Tuckett, C. M. *Christology and the New Testament: Jesus and His earliest Followers.* Louisville: Westminster John Knox, 2001.

Yarbro Collins, A. "Mark and His Readers: the Son of God among Greeks and Romans." *Harvard Theological Review* 93 (2000) 85–100.

———. "Mark and His Readers: the Son of God among Jews." *Harvard Theological Review* 92 (1999) 393–408.

7

The Disciples and Jesus

After Jesus, the most important persons in the Gospel are the disciples. They are the direct partisans of Jesus. In Mark's eyes, the deep significance of Jesus only appears in considering his relationship with the disciples. Through the disciples' attitude and their reactions, readers form not only a picture of them but also of Jesus. They perform the mirror function in which we can read the effects of the deeds and actions of Jesus. It is therefore important to make a deeper analysis of what they do or not do. To understand the role of the disciples is of major importance in order to analyze the reading experience. This springs among other things from the fact that the disciples form a group that will be present from the beginning to the end. It is a well-known phenomenon that readers—quite like spectators at the movies—willingly identify with one or other character in the story that unfolds before their eyes. This identification normally makes them choose people with which they feel sympathy. It seems that, in Mark, most readers identify with the disciples. This could be explained by the fact that these disciples are, after Jesus, the first people to appear in the story and that, thanks to their initially approving attitude to Jesus, they leave a positive impression. But this initial identification between the disciples and readers will not unfold according to a rectilinear process in the later developments of the narrative. Finally, to follow the narrative line of the disciples leads the readers to a confrontation with themselves.

The First Choice

Immediately after the synthesis of his message (Mark 1:14–15) Jesus first calls four disciples: Peter and Andrew, James and John. These are the first who find themselves near him and are invited to follow him. Readers will recognize the hand of the writer Mark in the narrative through the repetitions and doublets:

> Mark 1:16–20: As Jesus passed along the Sea of Galilee, he saw Simon and his brother Andrew casting a net into the sea—for they were fishermen. And Jesus said to them, "Follow me and I will make you fish for people." And immediately they left their nets and followed him. As he went a little farther, he saw James son of Zebedee and his brother John, who were in their boat mending the nets. Immediately he called them; and they left their father Zebedee in the boat with the hired men, and followed him.

The mission of these first disciples is not a small doing: to abandon goods and people to become "fishers of people." Moreover, the meaning of this latter activity is not even specified. The only setting to refer to in an attempt to grasp the meaning would be the summary of the program of Jesus in the preceding verses. There he mentions the closeness of the Kingdom of God and the consequences that it can involve for the behavior of human beings (conversion, faith in the gospel). The four thus become collaborators in this program. This passage, without the slightest break between the announcement of the Kingdom by Jesus and the call of the first disciples, is meant to stir up ideas and some expectations from the readers. First, Jesus' action is not an isolated fact. He did not come all alone to realize an individual goal and then disappear. It implies that his task is so immense that it will certainly need collaborators. Then, it seems that the coming of the Kingdom of God is not only the business of God, but also implies humans. It is entrusted to humans who will share the responsibilities and who will have to realize it with God. God and human beings are not separate or opposed. And finally, the eventual success of the disciples will depend on the extent of their commitment to Jesus. The call or the invitation to follow him means that they would have to try to understand how Jesus acts.

The disciples accede to the call of Jesus. We have a right to wonder why. Do we have to see in it Jesus' authority and put in doubt the freedom of the disciples? Or did these four fishermen prove to be naive? Did they perhaps have nothing to lose? Mark is not very precise and besides it is not very important. But the way in which the event is described can very well orient what follows for the reading experience. Everything unfolds quickly and without the least hesitation. A bit as if the scenario had been well established ahead of time. Biblical exegesis has given the name of "typical scene" or "ideal scenario" to the way this scene of the call of the first four disciples unfolds. It is not a factual event but a typical formulation of the way in which we can imagine the call of a disciple by Jesus. That's indeed what happens here. Jesus sees and calls. The disciple hears and follows. No other details. The called persons follow "immediately." By means of this ideal presentation, it is equally the readers who seem to be questioned. Here, from the beginning of the narrative, they face a choice. How do they judge the disciples? The answer to this question positions them also in relation to Jesus.

Readers are thus in a situation of decision. If they decide to pursue the reading, they express the desire in their turn to follow the disciples in order to know more about Jesus from them. And if all readers remain completely free to have their own viewpoint, the evangelist decides not to give to anyone reasons to disconnect at this stage of the narrative. He makes use of rhetoric to orient the interpretation of his readers. They can be absolutely confident to having made a good decision by pursuing the reading. That's because they know more than the disciples about Jesus. As they were able to read the prologue of the Gospel, they acquired—in relation to the disciples and every other person in the narrative—an advantage in knowledge: they were able to read from the first verse of the Gospel that Jesus is the Son of God. They were able to read that the Scriptures predicted him (Mark 1:2–4). They know that John the Baptist has designated him as a significant person (Mark 1:5–8). They realize that a voice came down from heaven to designate Jesus as the beloved Son (Mark 1:9–11). And they read how Jesus in the desert resisted the devil and finally conquered him (Mark 1:12–13). In this sense, readers decide on other bases than the disciples, because in following their reading, they follow not only Jesus but also the Son of God. Whatever the case may be, both of them—as much the readers who have been informed about the identity of Jesus as the disciples who must still discover who he is—are confronted in what follows in the narrative with the consequences of their choice. Disciples and readers advance hand in hand in the Gospel while a dialogue opens between them. Neither of the two parties is yet conscious of the risks that implies.

Presence

Mark has conceived his narrative in such a way that at the beginning of the Gospel, the choice of the readers is presented parallel with that of the disciples. They share an enthusiasm of the same kind. But then? Let's try to offer an explanation with the help of some reading experiments concerning the relationship between Jesus and the disciples. This relationship is constructed of diverse components. A first perspective is that of the tension between the presence and absence of disciples close to Jesus. Let's look at the presence first. There is a tension the evangelist wants to evoke. The call of the first disciples creates a narrative line of solidarity between Jesus and the disciples, a line that is pursued for a good time in the Gospel. Thus the group of disciples grows. First, and in the same way as for the first four disciples, Jesus calls the tax collector Levi. Jesus passes the lakeside and sees him at work. There follows Jesus' brief question and the positive reaction of Levi. This prolongs the ideal picture of the disciple:

> Mark 2:14: As he was walking along, he saw Levi son of Alphaeus sitting at the tax booth, and he said to him, "Follow me." And he got up and followed him.

Later he institutes the twelve (Mark 3:13–19). The motif of this institution is "to be his companions and send them to preach" (Mark 3:14). This institution comes after a summary that mentions Jesus' successes. People arrive from everywhere, he heals many sick people and casts out demons (Mark 3:7–12). The evangelist inserts this institution into his narrative at the right moment. He first of all tells that Jesus accomplishes several healings and exorcisms. That's why he exerts a huge attractive power over all the people who surround him. The moment has therefore come to involve more collaborators. The institution comes after a series of five conflicts between Jesus and his disciples on one hand and the religious authorities on the other. All collaboration in the spread of the Kingdom of God is thus welcome.

The presence of the disciples near Jesus is essential. It is the picture that spontaneously comes to the minds of the readers whenever they think of "being a disciple." The disciples are present when Jesus enters a synagogue or enters a city or town, which arouses in the readers the feeling that all goes well and that the disciples understand what matters to Jesus. Thus they are privileged witnesses to the spread of the Kingdom of God. And through the eyes of the disciples, readers also have access to the realizations of Jesus.

Later in the Gospel, the twelve will be sent (Mark 6:7–13) but the material distance between Jesus and the disciples does not involve for all that a separation between the two parties. During the course of their mission, the disciples remain mentally near Jesus. Haven't they received as a mission to do the same thing as he? Which they moreover do with full success:

> Mark 6:12–13: So they went out and proclaimed that all should repent. They cast out many demons, and anointed with oil many who were sick and cured them.

Jesus' success is not limited therefore to his own healings and exorcisms: the collaboration with his disciples seems completely fruitful also. According to the text, the disciples come back almost immediately after their mission and then remain close to Jesus. Even if the evangelist does not say with a maximum of clarity about this subject, readers could find here a key to understand what "fishers of people" means. The disciples do what Jesus does. Since it is a question about the meaning of the term "mission" ("he sent them out two by two") the idea of "fishers of people" has taken the form in the imagination of a lot of people of a kind of proselytism, synonymous with "winning souls" by convincing people of the truth of a certain belief. Now, it is not like that at all. The disciples are collaborators who announce the gospel by living it. If the good news is not welcomed and the disciples are not welcome, they have to abandon the place.

The Larger Circle of Jesus' Disciples

The fact that Jesus and the disciples seek to realize a similar program and that they succeed in doing it encourages the readers to have confidence in what Jesus does. From a literary viewpoint, the evangelist has succeeded in creating a unity between Jesus, the disciples, and the readers. Contrary to what the authorities do, the origin of the disciples is situated in popular villages, which gives an indication of the preferences of Jesus. With them, he almost never has discussion about questions of theology. He asks them to "repent" and he wants to team up with them to achieve what he has undertaken. The twelve seem to constitute a core, but it is completely plausible that Jesus has been surrounded by other people also that have followed him closely for a more or less long time. Thus we are informed at the end of the Gospel, when the masculine disciples are eclipsed, that there were also faithful women among his disciples:

> Mark 15:40–41: There were also women looking on from a distance; among them were Mary Magdalene, and Mary the mother of James the younger and of Joset, and Salome. These used to follow him and provide for him when he was in Galilee; and there were many other women who had come up with him to Jerusalem.

Even if the twelve seem to occupy a specific place and Jesus sometimes gives them a "private" teaching" (Mark 4:10, 34; 7:17–18; 10:10–11), other words of Jesus clearly suggest that anyone has the opportunity to go with him in his way of life. We have already drawn attention to the fact that Jesus considers all those who do the will of God as his brother, his sister or his mother (Mark 3:34b–35). Likewise, his teaching in the parables concerning the Kingdom of God is given in public and intended for the gathered multitude (Mark 4:1–2). The expression "Let anyone with ears to hear listen" is repeated several times and is addressed to all the people present (Mark 4:9, 23). Even his call to follow him is addressed to the multitude:

> Mark 8:34: He called the crowd with his disciples, and said to them, "If any want to become my followers, let them deny themselves and take up their cross and follow me."

This enlargement of the target group is not without impact on readers. Even without identifying with the twelve, they can feel called by Jesus' words. The message of the gospel is not something reserved for the few.

Failure to Understand Jesus' Words

Up to now, we have above all elucidated the positive relational line between Jesus, the disciples, and the readers. However, Mark does not need other people than the disciples to make alive another thing for the readers. It is not because the disciples are collaborators in the coming of the Kingdom that they understand everything about Jesus. Far from that. Scholars have long been able to state that the disciples selected by Jesus are not especially smart in the functions that have fallen on them. If they shine, it is rather in the negative. The distance between them and Jesus is hollowed out in the process as the narrative proceeds. The indication of alienation does not cease to increase. And once they realize this other aspect of things, readers become fascinated by it. Here are some of the elements.

The first failures in the relationship between Jesus and the disciples happen because of the disciples' lack of understanding in relationship to what Jesus says and does. Let's for a few moments make a distinction between actions and words, and let's focus first on the lack of understanding relative to words. Although his parables seem accessible to all, the disciples need explanations. And, in spite of them, unresolved questions remain in their heads. Indeed it happens on several occasions in the Gospel that Jesus feels obligated "in private" to furnish explanations of the words or acts, as is, for example, the case after his exposés about the clean and unclean or about divorce. In the light of what the readers have learned about the attitude of the disciples after the parable of the sower, you can see everything in this specific teaching about their lack of ability to understand Jesus.

> Mark 4:10–13: When he was alone, those who were around him along with the twelve asked him about the parables. [. . .] And he said to them, "To you has been given the secret of the kingdom of God, but for those outside, everything comes in parables."

> Mark 4:33–34: With many such parables he spoke the word to them, as they were able to hear it; he did not speak to them except in parables, but he explained everything in private to his disciples.

> Mark 7:17–18 (*following a teaching about clean and unclean*): When he had left the crowd and entered the house, his disciples asked him about the parable. He said to them, "Then do you also fail to understand? Do you not see that whatever goes into a person from outside cannot defile?"

> Mark 10:10 (*following a teaching about divorce*): Then in the house the disciples asked him again about this matter.

For the group that was closest to Jesus, it does not seem so simple to understand what he meant. For the disciples, the content of the message led to confusion. They had difficulty in understanding what Jesus meant by the nearness of the Kingdom of God. What it represented exactly escapes them. And to the extent that we go on in the Gospel, we perceive that Jesus and the disciples seem to have different perspectives about this Kingdom. For Jesus, the event of the Kingdom of God means that we have a different outlook on reality. It is what appears the most obviously during discussions about the identity of those who could enter the Kingdom: Who will be able to go in? Mark unites three of these discussions in chapter 10 and, in fact, all three bear on the reversal of the usual norms in force in the world to allow people to enter the Kingdom. I pick them up briefly by indicating the point of the debate.

A Question of Perspective

The first discussion has as its object the conditions of admission into the Kingdom (Mark 10:13–16). When people take children to Jesus, the disciples rebuke them because they pester Jesus. Seeing this, Jesus utters a revolutionary statement by placing a child as a model for those who desire to enter the Kingdom. At this time, children occupied a place at the very bottom of the social scale. Nevertheless, Jesus says:

> Mark 10:15: "Truly I tell you, whoever does not receive the kingdom of God as a little child will never enter it."

It is not a question here of a kind of romantic naiveté. Jesus' message is much too anchored in the reality of the everyday. It is rather an attitude of solidarity with those who do not have a place in society. Jesus associates himself with the image of God in the psalms and the prophets in which God sides with the little people. If that is the case, then they alone, along with those who identify with them, can enter the Kingdom.

The second discussion unfolds on the occasion of the question of the rich young man who seeks to "inherit eternal life" (Mark 10:17–31). He knows and perfectly observes the commandments, but Jesus asks for more, "One thing you lack, go, what you have, sell it to the poor and give it to the poor, and you will have treasure in heaven, then, come, follow me." Now the man was not able to abandon his goods. There again, Jesus starts from a clear perspective on the Kingdom of God. It is much more difficult for rich people to enter it *and* it is not enough to know the law. It is as if Jesus exhorts him to change his thinking. As long as we cling to the norms in force in the world to acquire riches and power, we cannot have access to the Kingdom. As his disciples are not bursting with enthusiasm, Jesus pursues the same subject with them. He gives a synthesis of what in his eyes can make possible this change of perspective: "For human beings, impossible, but not for God: because everything is possible for God."

The third discussion takes place among the disciples themselves, and the narrative illustrates in a striking way why the disciples do not understand Jesus (Mark 10:35–45). They have just been present in the scene with the children and with the meeting with the young man. But that does not prevent them from having a dispute about the places of honor that each of them will have in the kingdom. The question that launches the discussion is quite characteristic:

> Mark 10:35: James and John, the sons of Zebedee, came forward to him and said to him, "Teacher, we want you to do for us whatever we ask of you."

In fact, they have not yet understood that they are in the service of others and do not have to be preoccupied in the first place with their own interests. It is rather rare in the Gospel that the disciples no longer hide their plans: whereas Jesus never stops concentrating on the Kingdom *of God* and, through his word and his actions, freeing sick people, the poor, children, and the possessed, the disciples are still reflecting in terms of holders of *worldly* power.

These three conversations warn us against eventual misunderstandings about the meaning of the Kingdom of God. Many believers and unbelievers alike shrink the notion of the Kingdom of God to life after death. It is for later, for afterward. That produces effects in two senses. Sometimes people draw force from this idea because the Kingdom will compensate for what they had to submit to of evil and suffering down here. We will be recompensed up there, they say. The Kingdom of God is a consolation. Others vigorously criticize this conception because it turns us away from real problems in our world. The Kingdom of God risks being considered as a refuge or an alibi to do nothing to make a better world. But these three conversations in Mark well reveal that we cannot contrast the present and the future. Whatever we think about a Kingdom beyond death, the narrator insists on the fact that for Jesus the importance of choice in favor of the rule here and now must never disappear into the background. It is a matter of being now like children, abandoning your possessions now, becoming now a servant instead of being served. This change in perspective that is mentioned is called, in the terms of Jesus, "to repent." This is a word that readers recall from the *summary* at the beginning of the Gospel (Mark 1:14). To repent does not mean that we have to hope that everything will be better later. To repent means on the contrary that we must not place ourselves at the center of reality and life, but that we must begin to reflect on God's part in what must happen in this world. This cannot be lacking in consequences for the concrete way to face life.

Failure to Understand Jesus' Actions

Likewise for his actions, Jesus often stirs up more questions than answers from his disciples. The passage on the parables of the Kingdom of God is immediately followed by the well-known story of the calmed tempest (Mark 4:35–41). The anecdote has this in particular that it is the first time that Jesus intervenes in nature. Such stories, commonly called "nature miracles," are often events that suggest to contemporary readers that it is not really true history that is important to the author. But in the logic of the related world, miracles are produced as invitations to flesh out the question of Jesus' identity. We generally admit that these miracle stories saw the light of day only after Jesus' death and that they're the result of debates that occupied minds among the first groups of disciples. The story of the calmed storm is noteworthy. There are the uneasy disciples because the sea is turbulent. They are surprised that Jesus can calmly sleep. They awaken Jesus and Jesus orders the tempest to calm itself. To that end, he pronounces the same words as when he imposes silence on the demons: "Silence! Be quiet!" (Mark 4:39). At once, the problem is resolved. But what is striking then is that the tension has not disappeared. It is in some way reversed. When we might expect that the disciples would congratulate, praise, or thank their master, it seems that they are rather prey to doubt, incertitude, even "of a great fear." Jesus rebukes them for being disturbed in this way. For their part, they are seized with fear and wonder: "Who is this?" (Mark 4:41). Readers think that if there is a group of characters in the Gospel that should recognize Jesus, it is the disciples. Now this is not what happens in Mark. Whereas the disciples have gone very far along the road with Jesus—whereas they have followed him, whereas he has taken sides with them, whereas he has taught them in private, whereas they are part of his new family—it is surprising to state that there is something about Jesus they do not grasp. Jesus remains a stranger to them.

It is only the first little failure, but it solidly influences the atmosphere between Jesus and the disciples. There seems no longer any end to the series of situations in which the disciples do not understand what Jesus is doing. The little failure does not cease getting larger. Here are some characteristic examples. To begin with, there is an analogous situation on the lake with yet another tempest (Mark 6:45–52; see v. 48). This time, Jesus has charged his disciples to make the crossing by boat. They are alone because he has not gone with them. When a man, Jesus, comes toward them walking on the water, they think they have seen a ghost. They seem no longer to be able to recognize him. Once again, the story's point is not in the most "miraculous" aspect of the story, that is to say, in the fact that Jesus walks on water. The evangelist orients his narrative in such a way that the non-recognition of Jesus by his disciples becomes the real key of the story. The reason for which they do not recognize Jesus can seem surprising:

> Mark 6:51b–52: And they were utterly astounded, for they did not understand about the loaves, but their hearts were hardened.

To better understand the intentions of the evangelist, we have to recommend the (re)reading of the preceding passage of the miracle of the loaves (Mark 6:34–44). The narrator in fact connects these two stories: if the disciples had understood the miracle of the loaves, they would have recognized Jesus. These two events are a part of what is called "the loaves section" (Mark 6–8) in which the motifs of loaves and the lack of understanding of the disciples are associated. This connection is even more obvious through the repetition of the two miracles of the loaves, traditionally called the multiplication of the loaves. They are of major importance to the communication between the evangelist and his readers.

The Triangle: Jesus—Disciples—Readers

The two miracles of the loaves make up the most striking example of the use of a narrative doublet in Mark (Mark 6:34–44; 8:1–9). In reading Mark for the first time, we are struck upon finding an almost identical miracle story only two chapters apart. Basically, the two stories treat the same subject and the second appears as a useless repetition. They both tell that a huge crowd is fed with a few loaves and fish and at the end there remain food in abundance. There are only details that differ. In the first case—the best known version—it is a matter of five thousand people, five loaves, two fish, and twelve baskets of leftovers. In what concerns us here, it does not seem interesting to mention when and how exegesis tries to explain this phenomenon of the doublet. It is better not to limit ourselves to explanations implying the existence of two stories in the tradition before Mark, or pretending that one of the versions would be a later addition to the text of Mark. These explanations do not place enough value on the creativity of the narrator and, besides, grant too great a role to chance. The significance of this succession of two identical events is located in the communication between the narrator and his readers. The double narrative furnished to the narrator the opportunity to insist on the lack of understanding of the disciples.

If, in the first version, we can understand that the disciples ask how they could feed all these people,

> Mark 6:37: But he answered them, "You give them something to eat." They said to him, "Are we to go and buy two hundred denarii worth of bread, and give it to them to eat?"

we are right to say to ourselves that they still have not understood Jesus when they ask precisely the same question in the second narrative:

> Mark 8:4: His disciples replied, "How can one feed these people with bread here in the desert?"

The only conclusion is that the evangelist consciously looks for ways to insist on the lack of understanding of the disciples. It was already shown when Jesus walked on water and when the evangelist presented the lack of understanding about the story of the loaves as an argument to explain that the disciples do not recognize Jesus in the person who approaches the boat. But this is even more evident when, after the second miracle of the loaves, Jesus picks up the words of the evangelist on the lack of understanding and the hardness of their heart (Mark 6:52) and addresses the disciples in severe and reproachful terms:

> Mark 8:17–21: And becoming aware of it, Jesus said to them, "Why are you talking about having no bread? Do you still not perceive or understand? Are your hearts hardened? Do you have eyes, and fail to see? Do you have ears, and fail to hear? And do you not remember? When I broke the five loaves for the five thousand, how many baskets full of broken pieces did you collect?" They said to him, "Twelve." "And the seven for the four thousand, how many baskets full of broken pieces did you collect?" And they said to him, "Seven." Then he said to them, "Do you not yet understand?"

With this repetitive style in which we recognize our narrator, this text mentions a first moment of deep crisis in the relations between Jesus and the disciples. "Crisis" means that readers are in the process of correcting their picture of the disciples. Where they had at first spontaneous sympathy for them, they begin to put distance between them and the disciples because the latter lack constancy in their attitude to Jesus. The disciples' lack of understanding is part of the strategy of the narrator who wants to lead his readers to reflect on the person of Jesus. Why don't the disciples recognize Jesus? What is it that they should have recognized then? From their side, the readers seem convinced that they would have been able to answer this question. The prologue has in fact better informed them than the disciples on the person of Jesus. It remains to them to conclude that the disciples do not recognize that Jesus is the Messiah and Son of God. The lack of understanding is entirely about the identity of Jesus. Who is he therefore to be able to accomplish these miracles?

Indeed, these severe words about the disciples above all have the readers in view. We would be strongly tempted to write that, for the evangelist, the disciples *cannot* yet understand and confess that Jesus is the Messiah because he must fear that, basing themselves on incomplete information, readers make an erroneous picture of Jesus for themselves. Even having gone with Jesus closely, having heard the announcement of the Kingdom of God and having been present at the miracles, the disciples are not able to see that Jesus is the Messiah. If, from their side, readers have been well informed of the identity of Jesus, they now see themselves forced to ask themselves about their ability to correctly interpret what Mark means by "Jesus the Messiah." This narrative interpretation intended for the perspective of readers has the advantage of relativizing two difficulties with which the contemporary readers seem to be confronted. Indeed, it is true that some people disconnect when they read stories of nature miracles because they cannot have historical value. Moreover, other people consider that the behavior of the disciples is psychologically incomprehensible. In a reader perspective, the answer is that it is not a question here of history, but of intelligence and vision, not of the disciples but of the readers. The lack of understanding of the disciples has nothing to do with knowing whether they understand how the miracles could take place historically. This is a modern problem that is not on the agenda in the Gospel. What's in question here is the problem of knowing what *readers* think of Jesus.

Thus the theme of the lack of understanding of the disciples prepares for a turning point in the Gospel. From now on the evangelist will explain more openly why he does not allow the disciples to reach the idea that Jesus is the Messiah. "He said this openly" (Mark 8:32). In the eyes of the narrator, the question of knowing if Jesus is the Messiah cannot be separated from the question of knowing what kind of Messiah he is. We are midway through the Gospel and we have just reached a turning point, a hinge moment.

A Hinge Moment: Jesus' Question

It was inevitable that, after so much lack of comprehension and questions on the part of the disciples, Jesus would finally answer with a question, "But for you, who am I?" (Mark 8:29). If the question is addressed to the disciples, the narrative strategy of the evangelist means that it also reaches readers. Apparently in the name of the whole group, Peter replies, "You are the Christ." As to knowing how and why Peter happens to utter this profession of faith, that is one of the numerous lacunas in the narrative. The psychological approach could suggest the following responses: on the one hand, the severity of Jesus' words would have opened their eyes, but, on the other hand, the length of their stay with Jesus would be sufficient for them to finally recognize him for who he is. Sometimes the explanation is focused on the healing of the blind man at Bethsaida that immediately precedes this profession of faith (Mark 8:22–26). This is the only event between the severe rebukes that Jesus addresses to his disciples and Peter's profession, and it is moreover a remarkable story because it differs on one point from the usual model of healing miracles. In fact, Jesus does not succeed in healing the blind man on the first try. After a first laying on of hands, the man only half sees: he sees people as if they were trees walking. It is only after Jesus has placed his hands on the eyes of the blind man a second time that "the latter sees clearly." We read in it a symbolic meaning in the sense that the evangelist would have placed this story here to remind readers that even the disciples have difficulty "seeing him clearly." Like those of the blind man, their eyes only open by steps. They need two miracles of the loaves and must twice conquer their anguish about an event on the sea (the calming of the tempest and Jesus walking on the water). Thanks to the symbolism of the healing of the blind man, Peter understood that Jesus is the Messiah. As for me, I do not think there is a conclusive solution to this problem. I think that the main problem of this profession lies elsewhere.

The narrative itself does not propose a clear response to the question of knowing why Peter calls Jesus the "Christ." It is much more important to consider the fact that he said it and that—completely in the style of this Gospel—Jesus hastens to nuance this title. First, he forbids the disciples to speak of it to anyone. Then, he gives them explanations about the way in which he wants it to be understood. This will be the first announcement of the Passion:

> Mark 8:31–32: Then he began to teach them that the Son of Man must undergo great suffering, and be rejected by the elders, the chief priests, and the scribes, and be killed, and after three days rise again. He said all this quite openly. And Peter took him aside and began to rebuke him.

This is the first time that Jesus "openly" mentions the Passion and it seems obvious that the prohibition to speak of him as Messiah must be explained by his words about the Passion. The idea that the Messiah must "suffer much" happens as a shock, as much for the disciples as for readers, although readers could have previously raised a few indications suggesting that something disastrous could strike Jesus. The scribes have already fomented the plan to have him liquidated (Mark 3:5–6); at the time of the institution of Judas as one of the Twelve, the narrator artfully adds to it that he would be "the very one who will hand him over" (Mark 3:19); John the Baptist has already been killed (Mark 6:17–29). But in this case, it is Jesus himself who mentions his own suffering. Jesus' explanation about the suffering that awaits him leads us to one of the keys that allows us to decode this narrative. Suddenly, another illumination happens over what precedes. If it was impossible for the disciples to understand Jesus, it is because they quite simply do not have enough information. By explicitly treating the theme of suffering in the second part of the Gospel, the author knew how to create tension in his story. He has first of all obtained from the readers their recognition of the power and authority of Jesus and of his relationship with God. But in seeing the disciples' lack of understanding, readers feel well that they still lack precision about Jesus' identity. Mark obviously understands that the theme of suffering provokes an effect of unexpected shock, and in this way he prepares his readers. The question, however, that remains in suspense about this Gospel will be: "Is the picture of the Son of God reconcilable with that of a suffering human being?"

Jesus' Criteria Concerning the Kingdom of God

We have already said that the announcement of the Kingdom of God by Jesus implies a change of perspective about reality and about God. The difference between Jesus' vision and that of the disciples shows itself most clearly in their reaction to Jesus' first announcement of the Passion. Whereas readers could expect that the recognition of Jesus as the Messiah leads to a high point, the narrative takes a quite different turn. Instead of a "close harmony" between Jesus and Peter, a violent conflict is born. Peter in fact protests and begins to scold Jesus. At which Jesus admonishes Peter in terms that could not be clearer:

> Mark 8:33: "Get behind me, Satan! For you are setting your mind not on divine things but on human things."

The appellation "Satan" makes us think about the stay of Jesus in the desert where he was put to the test by Satan (Mark 1:12–13). Peter thus finds himself placed in the same category as Jesus' greatest adversary. This explains Jesus' anger but also that it is a matter here of an absolutely basic question in the Gospel. Jesus' argument contains the criterion in force in the Kingdom of God: accomplishing God's will and not that of human beings. Jesus concludes from the disciples' reaction that they are preoccupied above all with themselves and that they reject the idea of persecution to Jesus and thus to themselves. This first announcement of the Passion by Jesus is the beginning of a new section in the Gospel that will have Jesus' teaching to the disciples about the Passion as its main theme. In that section readers learn to know better the way Jesus thinks. We could define this section as an explanation of what "accomplishing God's will" can mean. This way of thinking is composed of an immense paradox that the disciples have all the trouble in the world to understand, let alone to accept!

By the way he elaborates this section the evangelist makes the readers feel acutely that it is serious business. Jesus says three times that he will have to suffer and be put to death. Three times, the disciples react with lack of understanding. As we have just seen, it is Peter who reacts the first time:

> Mark 8:32: And Peter took him aside and began to rebuke him.

The second time, the narrator explains:

> Mark 9:32: But they did not understand what he was saying and were afraid to ask him.

And the third time, James and John ask Jesus:

> Mark 10:35: "Teacher, we want you to do for us whatever we ask of you."

At each rejection of the disciples Jesus replies with explanations about the new logic of the Kingdom of God. These explanations contain the quintessence of the evangelical message. Here are a few extracts and a word of commentary:

> Mark 8:34–37: He called the crowd with his disciples, and said to them, "If any want to become my followers, let them deny themselves and take up their cross and follow me. For those who want to save their life will lose it, and those who lose their life for my sake, and for the sake of the gospel, will save it. For what will it profit them to gain the whole world and forfeit their life? Indeed, what can they give in return for their life?"

> Mark 9:35: He sat down, called the twelve, and said to them, "Whoever wants to be first must be last of all and servant of all."

> Mark 10:42–45: So Jesus called them and said to them, "You know that among the Gentiles those whom they recognize as their rulers lord it over them, and their great ones are tyrants over them. But it is not so among you; but whoever wishes to become great among you must be your servant, and whoever wishes to be first among you must be slave of all. For the Son of Man came not to be served but to serve, and to give his life a ransom for many."

These texts are of major importance in forming a judgment about Mark's narrative. They indeed contain what we call "the standards of judgment" that allow readers to have an opinion about what is happening in the story. These few verses give access to the criteria of judgment used by the evangelist to evaluate the people in the story. It is by leaning on these criteria that readers will examine the relationship between Jesus and his opponents, his disciples, his family, and all other people in the story. At the same time, these criteria hold up a mirror to readers. Once again, Jesus' words also put the readers' opinions in question.

To Be Continued

The Passion leads us to a new theme that moreover will perhaps also be the most important in Mark. We pick it up in a new chapter. But readers can here and now remember three questions: We know that up until now, *Jesus* makes his words follow his acts, but will this still be the case when he announces that he must suffer and die? How will *the disciples* react to what happens to Jesus? And what about the *readers*? Will this new and decisive moment of choice for or against Jesus who presents the announcement of the Passion be for them the time of giving up or continuing their reading?

For Further Reading

Best, E. *Disciples and Discipleship: Studies in the Gospel according to Mark.* Edinburgh: T. & T. Clark, 1986.

Baudoz, J.-F. *"Prendre sa croix." Jésus et ses disciples dans l'évangile de Marc.* Lire la Bible 154. Paris: Cerf, 2009.

Black, C. C. *The Disciples according to Mark: Markan Redaction in Current Debate.* JSNTSupp 27. Sheffield: JSOT Press, 1989.

Brandt, P.-Y. *L'identité de Jésus et l'identité de son disciple: le récit de la transfiguration comme clef de lecture de l'evangile de Marc.* NTOA 50. Freiburg and Göttingen: Vandenhoeck & Ruprecht, 2002.

Danove, P. "The Narrative Rhetoric of Mark's Ambiguous Characterization of the Disciples." *Journal for the Study of the New Testament* 70 (1998) 21–38.

———. "A Rhetorical Analysis of Mark's Construction of Discipleship." In *Rhetorical Criticism and the Bible*, edited by S. E. Porter and D. L. Stamps, 280–296. JSNTSupp 195. Sheffield: Sheffield Academic, 2002.

Driggers, I. B. *Following God through Mark: Theological Tension in the Second Gospel.* Louisville: Westminster John Knox, 2007.

Hanson, J. "The Disciples in Mark's Gospel: Beyond the Pastoral/Polemical Debate." *Horizons in Biblical Theology* 20 (1998) 128–57.

Kingsbury, J. D. *Conflict in Mark: Jesus, Authorities, Disciples.* Philadelphia: Fortress, 1989.

Shiner, W. T. *Follow Me! Disciples in Markan Rhetoric.* SBL Diss 145. Atlanta: Scholars, 1995.

Struthers Malbon, E. *In the Company of Jesus. Characters in Mark's Gospel.* Louisville: Westminster John Knox, 2000.

Thompson, M. R. *The Role of Disbelief in the Gospel of Mark: A New Approach to the Second Gospel.* New York: Paulist, 1989.

8

The Strength of Powerlessness

Introduction

In the section of the three announcements of the Passion, the evangelist describes how Jesus goes with full assurance to Jerusalem (Mark 8:27—10:52). Knowing what lies ahead, he nevertheless willingly pursues his path. The interpretation of this attitude of Jesus does not have unanimity among exegetes. We can indeed question ourselves about what Jesus is doing. Was he consciously looking to suffer? Did he know that he was going to come back to life and was this knowledge sufficient to get rid of fear? And if he had foreknowledge of all that, why didn't he do anything to flee this terrible fate? The question is even more passionate in that the first announcement of the Passion says explicitly that "the Son of man *must* suffer greatly" (Mark 8:31). Biblical experts have traditionally interpreted this verb "to have to" (in Greek *dei*) as a divine necessity. Jesus follows this path because it is God's will. From that time, it is not surprising that this interpretation has led a number of people to picture a cruel Christian God who desires the death of his own son. It is not possible in this context to go into depth into the universal problem of suffering, but let's emphasize even so that it is still way too frequent to hear the misunderstanding that Christianity has the solution to the problem of evil or suffering. The hypothesis that God would wish evil is not an option to hold on to. The way in which readers interpret suffering in Mark's narrative probably depend in large part on the opinion about suffering they have already previously formed, an opinion generally based on their own experiences. From his point of view, the evangelist scarcely gives transparent explanations about Jesus' suffering. This means that a great freedom is given to the readers to fill in the meaning of this suffering. For this chapter, my starting point is the idea that too often one reads the Gospel in a desire to find an answer to the "problem of suffering." This is an approach much too general for Mark's narrative, and that's why I am following the narrative line of the communication between the text and the reader.

Jesus, God, and Suffering

To thoroughly grasp the relationship between Jesus and God in relation to suffering, we must not isolate the chapters on Jesus' Passion from the rest of the Gospel. That God is concerned about Jesus' suffering should not surprise the reader who has read the *whole* text. The evangelist indeed presents Jesus and God as two partners from the beginning, partners concerned about a common cause. The actions and the words of Jesus are impregnated with God. His perspective on the world, on people, and on himself is rooted in the announcement of the arrival of the Kingdom of God. Twice, even, God will call Jesus his Son. If Jesus, however, refutes in public the title "Son of God," it is only to avoid the risk of being badly understood. And when the days approach in which Jesus must suffer, neither the evangelist nor Jesus sees in it a reason to erase God from the story of the life of the latter. On the contrary: the relationship between Jesus and God becomes only more intense.

I propose here three elements related to the relationship between Jesus and God. First, suffering is not lived as contrary to God's will. This is clearly different in comparison with the affirmation that God wishes suffering. From the narrative viewpoint, it is important that the readers realize that it is Jesus who pronounces the words "the Son of man must suffer" and not God or the opponents or the disciples. From Jesus' perspective (and that of the completely trustworthy narrator) God is an ally who advances toward death with him. Each step on the Jerusalem road Jesus-with-his-God draws nearer and nearer to death. Second, the relationship between Jesus and God never constitutes an obstacle for Jesus on the path of his own liberty. The evangelist insists on the fact that Jesus assumes his own responsibility. We saw above in the conversations with his disciples that Jesus supports himself with criteria that constitute a setting in which suffering can have a place. It is also in perfect inside knowledge that he places certain actions he knows will raise polemic and opposition. The outburst that he provokes in the temple by expelling money changers and sellers is a good example (Mark 11:15–19). The last meal that he has with his disciples is equally a sign of his freedom in acting (Mark 14:12–25). The fact of choosing this way himself sheds another light on this "divine necessity" that leads to Jesus' death. It would seem that, when Jesus approaches death, the expression functions as a warning signal addressed to the reader. It means that the latter must not think that the suffering and crucifixion of Jesus can be finally reduced to something normal and obvious. Attention to the suffering and death of Jesus, says the evangelist, shows that the current God is the same one who was there at the time Jesus healed the sick and told his parables. We must not try to eliminate this God when the wheel of fortune seems to have turned and Jesus' suffering begins.

The expression "divine necessity" moreover risks leading to confusion. It is theologically doubtful if we understand by this idea that God would have had the plan to send Jesus to death or that he had himself hung a sword of Damocles above his head. This "magical" reading of a transcendent being who makes human beings act on earth like in the theater of marionettes is far distant from the style of our evangelist. God is not guilty of the death of Jesus. We better understand the idea of "divine necessity" as a "translation" to a transcendent level of what has already taken place for a long time among the opponents of Jesus. The evangelist does not in fact delay too much in telling how these people begin to plot in order to eliminate Jesus. By taking the road to Jerusalem, Jesus sees himself faced with these plots. If, in this narrative, people are really responsible for the death of Jesus, the evangelist certainly does not point the finger at God, but at the collusion between the holders of religious and secular power.

It thus seems clear—and this is my third point—that "divine necessity" is the translation to the transcendent level of the freedom assumed by even Jesus himself to take the road to Jerusalem. It is not at all that he resents his life as if he were a robot in God's hands. The concern of the narrator is to make it so the reader well understands that the protagonist Jesus is absolutely convinced that in everything he undertakes he has God at his side. It was the same way in the first part of the Gospel, when Jesus proved that he had great liberty to act to reveal, contrary to the opinions of his adversaries, his own interpretation of the law. It is again still the same in the second part in which Jesus proves to have the same liberty in going to Jerusalem. The announcements of the Passion finally produce a double effect on readers. They draw attention once again to the authority of Jesus who, knowing the negative events that await him, does not let go for a moment of the reins of the action. Then—and we touch there the new, shocking revelation by the evangelist—God is not absent in suffering, just as he has never been absent in all that Jesus does.

In the explanation that Jesus gives to the disciples concerning the wisdom of life of the true disciple, we understood this famous paradox that "whoever wants to save their lives will lose them" (Mark 8:35). We now state that Jesus' wisdom is rooted in another paradox: the picture of Jesus' God and the freedom of the human being are in no way exclusive. For Jesus the freedom that he lives in God is the ultimate reason of his choice of the road to Jerusalem. True liberty in the Kingdom of God is to give one's life for others. It is only in this sense that we can understand the opposition that Jesus introduces in his reply to Peter when the latter has just shown his disapproval of suffering: "For you are setting your mind not on divine things but on human things" (Mark 8:33).

It is well worthwhile to add a remark that is not without importance. Readers must not forget the starting point of a narrative approach that a gospel takes up the narrator's interpretation on Jesus (an interpretation read in turn by the eyes of the guide-exegete). Consequently it is obvious that the interpretation mentioned says nothing about the historical trustworthiness of what unfolds in the mind of Jesus. The Gospel of Mark contains an elaborate construction by an author belonging to the second or third generation of Christians. Scholarship on the Gospels tells us that the picture of the four evangelists resembles at numerous points the historical person that could be Jesus, but that it is virtually impossible to precisely reconstruct what Jesus could say or do. It is probable that the three announcements of the Passion have been written later in the light of the way the first followers then envisaged the death of Jesus. The challenge before the readers is to conceive their own way of envisaging the story of Jesus such as Mark tells it.

Jesus Dies Alone

By expressing too many theoretical and theological considerations on suffering, we risk losing from sight that the evangelist himself scarcely theorizes about the meaning of Jesus' death. That's annoying enough for exegetes. As part of their profession, they invest a maximum of energy into the understanding and explanation of the theology of the evangelist. But the evangelist in quest forcefully leads them in another direction because, for him, the real meaning of Jesus' death is not so much a question of understanding as doing. The Gospel of Mark is a "practical" gospel. It has in view the involvement of the readers. Even when it comes to suffering. From that it is completely normal that the evangelist concentrates in the first place on the reaction of the people in the company of Jesus. And we inevitably find the two principal groups that we have previously mentioned, that of the adversaries and that of the disciples. These two groups are in agreement in that they both harden their positions as the denouement is approaching.

The *adversaries* of Jesus are still more firmly opposed and finally decide to liquidate him by whatever means. Beginning in chapter 12, scribes, high priests, elders, Pharisees, Sadducees, and Herodians enter into a pact with the intention of finding any motive whatever to accuse Jesus and to arrest him. In the end, they seek to obtain the necessary collaboration of the occupying Roman who only has the right to put him to death. Then the events succeed each other one after the other and the evangelist describes with a lot more precision than usual their succession and their coherence. More or less a third of the Gospel is dedicated to the seven last days of Jesus' life. As for the religious opponents' attitude to Jesus, we can only understand it if we are conscious that it does not even come to their mind that Jesus could be the Son of God. Their reflection strictly follows the lines of their traditional conception of the law, which moreover are often very different between them. In their picture of God, there is no place for a "spoil-sport" like Jesus, who unmasks the weak points of their system. On the other hand, the narrator has furnished readers all the opportunities so that they can sympathize with Jesus' picture of God. Duly informed by the narrator about the true identity of Jesus, readers consider the actions of the adversaries with a touch of irony—opponents who seek at all costs to put an end to the career of Jesus and for whom it is in fact child's play to get rid of him. But readers perfectly perceive that their triumph is in reality a defeat. They do not know whom they have killed and they do not know as well that this death is not the end for Jesus. From the adversaries' viewpoint, it is they who are the great victors, and the death of the blasphemer Jesus has likewise put an end to his story. But the narrator and readers expect what follows. They remember in fact that the announcements of the Passion by Jesus end each time with words about the resurrection.

> Mark 8:31: Then he began to teach them that the Son of Man must undergo great suffering, and be rejected by the elders, the chief priests, and the scribes, and be killed, *and after three days rise again*."

> Mark 9:31: [. . .] for he was teaching his disciples, saying to them, "The Son of Man is to be betrayed into human hands, and they will kill him, and three days after being killed, *he will rise again*."

> Mark 10:34: [. . .] and he began to tell them what was to happen to him, "[. . .] they will mock him, and spit on him, and flog him and kill him; *and after three days he will rise again.*"

These prophecies bring us back to the *disciples* to whom they were intended. The attitude of the disciples likewise hardens. If we could say that, before Peter's profession of faith, they *could not* understand Jesus, in the second part of the Gospel it seems rather that they do not *want to understand him*. We know their reaction to the three announcements of the Passion: they refuse to admit that Jesus will have to suffer. In this sense, readers will be more or less surprised to learn that they nevertheless follow him on the road to Jerusalem. Peter—him again—even gives the impression that he has indeed understood, in the name of all the others, what Jesus has explained:

> Mark 14:27–31: And Jesus said to them, "You will all become deserters; for it is written, 'I will strike the shepherd, and the sheep will be scattered.' But after I am raised up, I will go before you to Galilee." Peter said to him, "Even though all become deserters, I will not." Jesus said to him, "Truly I tell you, this day, this very night, before the cock crows twice, you will deny me three times." But he said vehemently, "Even though I must die with you, I will not deny you." And all of them said the same.

But, beginning from this moment, the disciples seem to have lost their bearings. Contrary to their words, they prove by their actions that they are obviously turning away from Jesus. Jesus asks them to watch and pray and he finds them asleep. Judas betrays Jesus and associates himself with an armed band to point him out. In the confusion of the arrest of Jesus, the evangelist notes:

> Mark 14:50: All of them deserted him and fled.

Here is Jesus alone. If Peter follows him again for a moment—and "from a distance"—he denies three times that he knows Jesus (Mark 14:54, 66–72). We cannot imagine a contrast more striking between the beginning and the end of narrative line concerning the disciples. What seemed to have begun as a story of success done with more and more enthusiasm and responsibility ends in a total fiasco. The call to join Jesus was only achievable as long as their own life was not really in play. If we had to evaluate the disciples on the basis of the criteria of the Kingdom of God, they would really be the last in the class, even failures. They want to save their life, dominate, and be the greatest and the first. They are not disposed to bear their cross and serve. The relationship between Jesus and the disciples seems to have ended in a tunnel and every question is to know if there is still a little light at the end, if they could still get out of this tunnel. For readers, the only lifeline comes to them from the three announcements of the Passion that we have just recalled and that all three include the resurrection on the third day. But will this resurrection really take place? Does this saying leave open the door for a renewed meeting between Jesus and the disciples? In a rather brief note, the narrator suggests that everything is still possible. . . .

> Mark 9:9–10: As they were coming down the mountain, he ordered them to tell no one about what they had seen, until after the Son of Man had risen from the dead. So they kept the matter to themselves, *questioning what this rising from the dead could mean.*

Jesus' Life and Death Are Well Matched

The majority of commentators consider the suffering and death of Jesus as the culminating point of the story. We know, for example, this aphorism from the nineteenth century according to which Mark's Gospel is a long Passion story with an introduction. The place of honor in this culminating point goes back to the words of the centurion at the foot of the cross:

> Mark 15:39: "Truly this man was God's Son!"

The real identity of Jesus is publicly revealed at the moment of his death on the cross. It is therefore exact that the intrigue of the story finds its denouement in Jesus' crucifixion. But if we take the trouble to read Mark in its totality, we retain a much more balanced picture. The meaning of the Passion comes to the surface only if we associate it with the first part of the Gospel. God is revealed as much in the words and actions of Jesus as in his suffering and death. Or, conversely, the condition allowing us to see God's presence in the agonizing Jesus is that we recognize him also in the liberating words and acts by Jesus during his lifetime. The two parts of the Gospel are complementary. To focus only on the death of Jesus constitutes an erroneous narrowing of the Gospel. The innovative aspect of the evangelist Mark (for example, in comparison with the epistles of Paul that were written earlier) is that he integrates Jesus' Passion into his life.

For the narrator, the way Jesus traverses this phase of suffering in his life is only the logical development of his earlier announcement of the coming of the Kingdom of God. The life and equally the death of Jesus show how God's action is liberating, which we only succeed in imagining if we allow preconceived pictures of God to fall away. Through exorcisms and healing Jesus presents a new picture of God. It was not a matter of the effects of a superior strength attributed to a kind of Superman who wanted to have himself recognized as God, but of signs of the nearness of God to human beings. The meaning of Jesus' death on the cross is of the same order. It is not a matter of the manifestation of an untouchable hero of such strength that he endures the worst suffering without flinching, but it is the phase in which God is revealed to the world in a broken human being. This reading also explains why the narrator insists so much on the irreducible aspect of the hostile behavior of the adversaries and on the lack of ability of the disciples to follow Jesus. One group as much as the other is impervious to the new picture of God that is inserted into the world through Jesus. They in fact are both, but in different ways, as conservative as the other. The reason for it is sufficiently obvious: the picture of the God of Jesus is revolutionary—so revolutionary that the evangelist cannot prevent himself from mentioning that Jesus himself encounters a crisis. In the very heart of suffering, the narrator insists very strongly on the human character of Jesus. Several hours before his death Jesus prays:

> Mark 14:36: He said, "Abba, Father! For you all things are possible; remove this cup from me; yet, not what I want, but what you want!"

And at the moment he dies, he cries out:

> Mark 15:34: *"Eloi, Eloi, lema sabachthani,"* which means, "My God, my God, why have you forsaken me?"

Here certainly are last words that are not very soothing! And again, they represent a true challenge to the reader. Here's a situation in which trust in God and the absence of God coincide. Does there really exist a God at the moment in which a human being cries out in the deepest of his misery, "My God! Where are you?"? For readers who have proved their tenacity by reading until the death of Jesus on the cross, these words have badly healed in their flesh. Because it is not a matter of the theoretical question of knowing if there can exist "a God" when "a human being" dies, but of Jesus addressing "my God" to whom he has devoted his whole life.

Jesus: The Reader's Revolutionary View of God

Our age and the media have spoken a lot about books that supposedly overturn the origins of Christianity and promise to reveal the real personality of Jesus. They pretend that, for many centuries, Christians would have leaned on the "wrong" texts as a basis of their belief. Every time the publication of a gnostic text or an apocryphal gospel provokes a backlash, because it creates the impression that the canonical narratives of the New Testament have not given the real picture of the authentic Jesus. After our reading, the question is to know if it is not the narrator of the Gospel of Mark who has unleashed the real revolutionary dynamite into the world. Who among us can indeed imagine a God in the human being Jesus agonizing on the cross? Who can imagine a God so "human, too human"?

In the thought of a very great number of people, God is a kind of superpower disposing of all possible powers, or almost . . . Some turn away from him because they feel he is a threat, others need this God because they feel weak. But the picture is the same for these two groups: it is that of an archaic God (Marie Balmary) an all-powerful God who takes away suffering, who fills in gaps in knowledge, or who punishes wickedness. In conceiving of such a God, we imagine him as being useful. But with Jesus, a new picture of God rises to the surface. The power of God is in solidarity with the powerless. That was the way Jesus thought when he announced the coming of the Kingdom of God. The fact of paying attention to people located on the margin of society is not the fruit of chance but his perfectly conscious choice. The choice to live his life according to this new criterion: the one who loses his life will save it. In the announcement of the Kingdom of God by Jesus, God is no longer the useful solution in the domains that go beyond human beings. He is precisely in human beings themselves who seek to be the most humble and the servant of all. In Mark's eyes, it is not possible for God to become more human than in the person of Jesus crucified. More than all the other evangelists, Mark can strongly associate himself with the theology of the death of God, although he would without any doubt have preferred the expression "theology of the death of the picture of God." The image of a powerful God had indeed become—and is still—an idolatrous image.

The Hermeneutic of Golgotha and the Readers

Jesus dies alone. We do not find any trace of any other character in the narrative beside him. But the narrator's strategy means that those readers who persevere find themselves at the very foot of the cross. For them, it is the hour of truth. At this point they are ready to some extent to cast a look back at the whole Gospel. But how will they react? How will they answer the question of Jesus: "And according to you, who am I?" How will they understand the call of Jesus inviting them to lose their lives in order to save them? How do they judge the behavior of the disciples who flee, betray and deny Jesus? In brief, what will they do?

In the eyes of readers who know that they are confronted with the message and the fate of Jesus, the Gospel according to Mark cannot remain a theoretical book. Jesus does not ask the disciples to take *his* cross for him. He asks them to follow their own route. It is not sufficient for the disciples of Jesus to get good grades in the knowledge of Jesus' teaching. It will be much more important to say no to themselves and in all liberty to take the way of the servant. The Gospel contains a specific hermeneutic that functions uniquely in the practice of life, a hermeneutic of Golgotha (L. E. Keck) in which Jesus' disciples give themselves to gain their life. It is a thing that's impossible to understand if you do not live it. It is impossible to understand the paradox of the servant at the theoretical level. It is only in the practice of self-denial that disciples could feel to what extent the Gospel of the Kingdom of God produces effects. This code functions as an instruction for those who read the Gospel of Mark. One person, Jesus, lived this experience, and Mark wrote down his story for the benefit of each of the readers.

Jesus followed this code until the end. Jesus is dead. And now?

The Paradoxical Message of Mark for the Reader

Each of these three paradoxes is placed in the context of an announcement of the Passion and resurrection (Mark 8:31; 9:31; 10:32–34) and of an anecdote on the lack of understanding of these announcements by the disciples (Mark 8:32; 9:32–34; 10:35–40). However, through Jesus' teaching, they learn that his Passion is "simply" the consequence of a certain perspective on life that can only be expressed in a paradoxical way. You do not have to wait until persecution or crucifixion take place to have the experience of these paradoxes. They can be lived here and now as a total reversal of the values of the world. What's important in the eyes of the world (authority, power, greatness, riches . . .) is worthless in the Kingdom of God. Just before the third announcement of the Passion and resurrection (Mark 10:32–34) and after the meeting with the rich young man (Mark 10:17–27) Jesus once again gives a teaching (Mark 10:29–31) to Peter and other disciples. The scene ends with a paradoxical word that functions as an encouragement or rather a warning to the disciples, "Many of the first will be last and the last will be first" (v. 31). Once again, it is a very concrete illustration of the way in which losing your life can lead to saving it. The paradoxes are not only anticipations of the theme of the cross and resurrection, they are also actualizations or realizations of this same theme in the concrete life of all those who follow Jesus after his death. These three paradoxes of service contain a wisdom that illustrates the very heart of the Gospel. Even if they are connected to the theme of the cross and suffering, their meaning is not limited to crucifixion or martyrdom. The paradox offers us a code to live the human relationships of everyday in the community. By beginning with the episode of Peter's confession (Mark 8:29) the disciples continually resist Jesus' thoughts. The fundamental reason for which, on several occasions, they do not understand his teaching, is clarified: each time that the message of the Passion is announced to the disciples, the reader learns that Jesus is obliged to give them a teaching on service.

What Does "Save Your Life" Mean?

In the paradoxes that we have encountered, there is a tension between two opposite poles. The negative pole (losing your life, being the servant and slave of all, being the last) is opposed to the positive pole (saving your life, being the greatest, being the first). If the meaning of the negative part is clear enough, we can wonder how the reader could trust in the real transformation of the negative pole into a positive pole. Is there any guarantee? The answer—the only reply—of Mark is at the level of the relationship between Jesus and God. To understand the meaning of paradoxes in concrete life, we thus have to return to what we said above about Jesus' identity. The relationship of Jesus with God is a basic line and a fundamental cornerstone of Mark's narrative. Without this line, the narrative loses its dynamism, its meaning and its suspense. We have seen that it is widely admitted that the Gospel according to Mark is characterized by an almost transparent veil that covers the relationship between Jesus and his God. No human person in Mark's narrative recognizes the real dimensions and consequences of this relationship. And the narrator invites readers to explore the text and to read between the lines until they find the key to understand the mystery (which does not imply moreover that this exploration can ever reach its end). It is precisely this paradoxical dimension of the characterization of Jesus as *suffering Son of God* that sheds its light on the concrete paradoxes and that helps the reader understand the tension and the unity of the two parts of each paradox. In the first place, Jesus is a trustworthy character because he completes the promises that he has made when he spoke of losing his life and becoming a slave of all. In the second place, he does not ask any remuneration for himself from it, but he shows a total trust in God who alone is capable of completing the second part of the paradoxes and makes him the first and greatest. As a consequence, the true denouement of Mark's narrative is not the cross but the empty tomb, in which the young man dressed in white proclaims, "He has been raised, he is not here" (Mark 16:6). In all its brevity, this is a victorious sentence that doubly gives meaning to the paradoxes of Mark 8:35; 9:35b and 10:43–44. First, in a condensed way, the paradoxes become illustrations of the christological paradox in its totality: God is on the side of the crucified man of Nazareth. The true greatness of Jesus is to be great in God's eyes. Second, because of the resurrection of Jesus, the "wisdom" of the paradoxes is not a call to absurdity or masochism. That's why we can never neglect that the three paradoxes follow three announcements of the Passion *and resurrection.*

For Further Reading

Balmary, M. *Freud jusqu'à Dieu.* Paris: Actes Sud, 2010.

Beck, R. R. *Nonviolent Story: Narrative Conflict Resolution in the Gospel of Mark.* Maryknoll, NY: Orbis, 1996.

Focant, C. "Verite historique et verite narrative: Le recit de la Passion in Marc." In *Bible et histoire: ecriture, interpretation et action dans le temps*, edited by M. Hermans and P. Sauvage, 83–104. Le livre et le rouleau 10; Connaitre et croire 6. Brussels: Lessius, 2000.

Keck, L. E. *Who Is Jesus? History in Perfect Tense.* Studies on Personalities of the New Testament. Columbia: University of South Carolina, 2000.

McKnight, S. "Jesus and His Death: Some Recent Scholarship." *Currents in Research: Biblical Studies* 9 (2001) 185–228.

Oberlinner, L. *Todeserwartung und Todesgewissheit Jesu: Zum Problem einer historischen Begründung.* Stuttgarter Biblische Beiträge 10. Stuttgart: Katholisches Bibelwerk, 1980.

Santos, N. F. *Slave of All: The Paradox of Authority and Servanthood in the Gospel of Mark.* JSNTSupp 237. Sheffield: JSOT Press, 2003.

Schmidt, U. "Zum Paradox vom 'Verlieren' und 'Finden' des Lebens." *Biblica* 89 (2008) 329–51.

Van Oyen, G. "The Vulnerable Authority of the Author of the Gospel of Mark: Re-Reading the Paradoxes." *Biblica* 91 (2010) 161–86.

Vouga, F. *Politique du Nouveau Testament: Leçons contemporaines.* Essais Bibliques. Geneva: Labor et Fides, 2008.

9

Epilogue: Where Is Jesus?

God's Answer

> Mark 16:1–8: When the sabbath was over, Mary Magdalene, and Mary the mother of James, and Salome bought spices, so that they might go and anoint him. And very early on the first day of the week, when the sun had risen, they went to the tomb. They had been saying to one another, "Who will roll away the stone for us from the entrance to the tomb?" When they looked up, they saw that the stone, which was very large, had already been rolled back. As they entered the tomb, they saw a young man, dressed in a white robe, sitting on the right side; and they were alarmed. But he said to them, "Do not be alarmed; you are looking for Jesus of Nazareth, who was crucified. He has been raised; he is not here. Look, there is the place they laid him. But go, tell his disciples and Peter that he is going ahead of you to Galilee; there you will see him, just as he told you." So they went out and fled from the tomb, for terror and amazement had seized them; and they said nothing to anyone, for they were afraid.

In the last words of Jesus on the cross, God seems not to be found. Only God in person could still answer. But does God reply to this cry? It is surprising to notice that the narrator gives so little attention to what follows in the story when, in Christian tradition, the resurrection is specifically imposed as the heart or even the neuralgic point of faith. The end of the book of Mark looks like a brief appendix of eight verses about an empty tomb. Not a word on the appearances of the resurrected Christ. However, this narrative marks with its imprint everything that goes before it because it expresses God's answer to Jesus' death. "He is raised, he is not here," a young man all dressed in white says. That's the confirmation that Jesus was definitely right when he announced this resurrection earlier in the Gospel. For a deed done there is no remedy, says popular wisdom. But this time it is obviously contradicted. If Jesus' death had seemed to announce a definitive end, this very death seems to bear in itself the germ of a new beginning. What's happening exactly in this case?

The End of the Narrative and the Reader

At the end of the Gospel, once again, the active role of the readers in the construction of meaning needs to be emphasized. Indeed, we could do a reading of Mark's Gospel beginning with the ending of Mark 16:1–8. The enterprise does not necessarily surprise because, to understand Mark's Gospel, we have to understand the ending of it and more particularly his perspective on the resurrection. The narrative ends with an open ending: the author does not tell if the disciples meet Jesus in Galilee. But there are at least three indications in the text that point to the real readers' responsibility to continue to "write" the Gospel.

The first point is the unity of verses 7 and 8. In the mind of the reader, these two verses create an incontestable opposition. Verse 7 contains an optimistic message and is full of hope, whereas verse 8 represents its opposite, made of fear, flight, and silence. This has led New Testament scholars to two different interpretations. According to some, we have to end the narrative positively, come what may, and strive to safeguard the *good news* of the Gospel. They put verse 7 in the center, and they minimalize and relativize the fear and silence of the women. But nothing makes us presume that the silence of the women is provisional or limited to those who are not disciples. According to others, we have to take the negative conclusion literally. They give all the weight to verse 8. Indeed, neither visual experience (the empty tomb) nor the auditory experience (the message of the young man) was able to convince the three women at the tomb of the good news of the resurrection. What are we to do? In my eyes, an exegesis that does not try to excuse the negative reaction of the women seems to take the text more seriously. Evidently, by accepting this negative interpretation, the abrupt ending of Mark becomes much more problematic, because if the look remains hung up on the negative reaction of the women in verse 8, the narrative risks becoming "a fabrication of the narrator who betrays himself through the inconsistency of his report."[1] There remains a third possibility that goes back to the combination of the positive pole with the negative. This interpretation consists first of freeing verse 8 from its isolation and of joining it to verse 7. We thus obtain a reading that corresponds to a literary technique that we already encountered. If we seek to understand the meaning of the reaction of the women (v. 8) with the message given previously by the young man (v. 7) the typical schema of "promise (divine)—failure (human)" can be useful to us. This pattern comes up on several occasions, notably when the announcements of the Passion and resurrection said by Jesus (Mark 8:31; 9:31; 10:32–34: the promises) are not understood by the disciples (Mark 8:32–33; 9:32–34; 10:35–41: failure). But each time, these moments of lack of comprehension are followed by a new and paradoxical catechesis given by Jesus, which shows that failure is not the last word of the schema. Thus, it is a schema in three stages. In Mark 16:7b and 16:8, we again find the sequence of the two first steps in which the promise ("Jesus goes before you to Galilee") is followed by a negative reaction (fear, flight, silence).

It is certainly not surprising that the recognition of this schema, and more particularly the absence of the third stage, contributes to showing the role of the readers. The participatory function on the part of the readers is well described by Driggers: "The future has been refused by characters but not by the Gospel's hearers."[2] The story demands to be continued, but since there is no continuation by and for the characters in the Gospel, only one person can continue it: the reader. "After such a finale, the question, 'What's going to happen in the story of the reader?' is much more relevant than that of the former story of the protagonists of the gospel."[3] In addition, our analysis of the schema has shown in what the activity of the readers will

1. Benoît Standaert, "Raconter la résurrection: Un Paradoxe narrative," in R. Bieringer, V. Koperski and B. Lataire, eds., *Resurrection in the New Testament,* Festschrift J. Lambrecht, Bibliotheca Ephemeridum Theologicarum Lovaniensium 156 (Louvain: Peeters, 2002) 73–91, esp. 78.

2. I. B. Driggers, *Following God through Mark: Theological Tension in the Second Gospel* (Louisville: Westminster John Knox, 2007) 94.

3. C. Focant, "Un silence qui fait parler (Mc 16,8)," in A. Denaux, ed., *New Testament Textual Criticism and Exegesis,* Festschrift J. Delobel, Bibliotheca Ephemeridum Theologicarum Lovaniensium 161 (Louvain: Peeters, 2002) 79–96 = *Marc, un évangile éetonnant: Recueil d'essais,* Bibliotheca Epheridum Theologicarum Lovaniensium 194, (Louvain: Peeters, 2006) 342–58, esp. 353.

consist: they must not seek to *understand* the empty tomb nor the resurrection as an "event" of the past, but they must rather *act* in the future. They must go in search of Jesus, because that's the only promise in the words of the young man that is not fulfilled. Since the women kept silent, readers are the only "disciples" to have heard the promise of the young man. After Jesus' death both disciples and readers live in quest of Jesus in everyday life.

The Women in Mark 16:1–8 and the Reader

The responsibility of readers in the process of continuing the narrative is equally revealed by the confrontation with the behavior of the women. Indeed, the characterization of the women is the second argument of narrative exegesis that points to the role of readers. At the level of characters, it is the presence of the women that creates the connection between the narrative of the empty tomb on the one hand and the crucifixion and the placing in the tomb (Mark 15:40–41, 47) on the other. Through this uninterrupted presence they become the protagonists of the last pericope. A function of hinge that cannot be underestimated. It is they who make the narrative advance. Spontaneously, after reading that they were present at the time of the crucifixion and at the placement in the tomb, readers will follow their travel to the tomb, placing their confidence in them. In Mark 15:41, Mark portrays the women in a positive way: they have already followed and served Jesus in Galilee. In addition, readers have learned to have more confidence in the minor characters, especially if, like the women, they are distinguished from the disciples, in a positive contrast. However, from Mark 16:1 on, these same readers will be obliged to distance themselves from the women because of an ambiguity: they left to anoint the body of Jesus but this anointing had already been done beforehand (Mark 14:3–9). Thus they arrive late. This ambiguity will change to a negative attitude in the final section (Mark 16:5c–8). The characterization of the women in the final pericope unfolds fully in a mixture of emotions, hope, and frustration, as much in them as in the readers, except that the women and the readers react differently as the narrative progresses. The readers and the women have the same information, but whereas for the readers this information confirms the good news of the resurrection, it becomes for the women a source of fear that ends up in silence and flight. In sum, in the perspective of the narrator, the women set out en route to look for a corpse, in a philosophy diametrically opposed to what the narrator has created for the readers. And nowhere in the story is there the slightest beginning of a positive change from this perspective.

A comparison between the behavior of the women and that of the disciples in the Gospel of Mark shows that the two groups testify to a similar attitude. The two do not seem to understand the message of the resurrection, that it is in the form of a promise (the disciples) or in the form of proclamation (the women). The typology of the women is thus identical to that of the disciples. In this context, we have to reread Mark 9:9. After the "transfiguration" on the mountain in which the disciples saw Jesus in his glory, he forbids them to speak of this experience but explicitly limited this prohibition: "only when the Son of man would be raised from the dead." They respect this prohibition, but they do not understand the note about the resurrection.

Commandment: Mark 9:9 be silent before the resurrection	*Commandment:* Mark 16:7 speak after the resurrection
Answer: positive action; obedience of the disciples	*Answer:* no action; disobedience of the women
Effect: failure to understand the resurrection	*Effect:* fear, silence, flight

Throughout the Gospel, the disciples never give the impression of understanding what Jesus says about the resurrection. Similarly, the women, placed by the narrator in a privileged state in the very place in which they could have seen and understood the resurrection of Jesus (the stone that was rolled away, the young man in white, his message) are not more capable of grasping the message of the resurrection.

The characterization of the women, identical to that of the disciples, is another revealing indication that readers must themselves continue the narrative. In the Gospel of Mark, the women do not have the function of a witness. Then who will witness if not the readers? Once again: the readers are the only ones who can to some extent pursue the narrative. This analysis of the characterization obligates us to look more closely at the third indication of the essential function of the readers in the elaboration of meaning.

Jesus, the Crucified, Resurrected One

We have explained how Mark wants to pass on the message of the resurrection to readers through a literary process and characterization. Can we say anything more about the author's perspective? To better understand his viewpoint, we could look from closer up how he presents his protagonist Jesus for the last time. There are two paradoxical dyads we can construct from the text. On the one hand, Jesus is at the same time the crucified and the resurrected. On the other hand, he is the absent one and the present one in the form of promise.

First, there is the unity "crucified—resurrected." The aspect of the Passion has always been recognized as being at the heart of the Gospel. To accept Jesus' Passion poses a problem for the disciples and the Passion is probably at the base of the messianic secret (Mark 8:27–33). But the great importance of the Passion also influences a correct understanding of the resurrection. It is not a victory that suppresses suffering and pain. On the contrary, there's always an inseparable unity between the Passion and resurrection. It is not an exaggeration to say that the Passion is a "necessary" part to understand the resurrection. To give only a single example, Elian Cuvillier has well shown that the lack of understanding of the disciples about the resurrection of the dead in Mark 9:9 is explained by the fact that they see the resurrection as

> a happy end, a solution to the failure of death. [. . .] Now for Mark, the resurrection of the Son of man means that he fully reveals himself in death. [. . .] That is what Mark wants to recall to his auditors, of whom the disciples are a figure: the glorious manifestation of the Transfiguration does not say everything about the identity of Jesus; he must be resurrected, i.e. he must pass through death, and that's just what is going to be the essential thing.[4]

According to the evangelist, the unity between the Passion and the resurrection was already present in the preaching of Jesus in the Gospel, thus in a pre-Easter perspective. The unity is rather located at the level of theology and existential experience than chronology.

It is not surprising therefore that the readers perceive the same paradox in the last pericope of the gospel, but then in a post-Easter perspective.

4. E. Cuvillier, "La résurrection dans l'évangile de Marc ou: La final court . . . et puis avant?" in D. Marguerat, ed., *Quand la Bible se raconte,* Lire la Bible 134 (Paris: Cerf, 2003) 105–22.

Verse 5 identifies the resurrected as the one who has been crucified: "You are looking for Jesus of Nazareth, who was crucified. He has been raised." It is obvious that this identification goes beyond categories of the usual representation of a human being. He is changed, and he is the same. Through the omission of all forms of the appearance of the resurrected Christ because of the abrupt ending, the Gospel according to Mark highlights, more than the other gospels, that the new mode of existence of Jesus will not be the object of a physical experience or a meeting with the same person. We must rather say that "the deep meaning of the resurrection of Christ appears in the *revelatory* dimension of his earthly life."[5] The past has an essential function to understand the new mode of existence. But on the concrete mode of the presence of the Christ, Mark creates a mystery instead of giving a definitive answer. The ending does not resolve anything; it continues to present Jesus in the same way as before, as the great unknown who is recognized by no one. The disciples and the women have left the scene. Once again, it belongs to the readers to seek to understand . . .

Jesus, the Absent One Present

The second tension created by Mark at the end of his Gospel is that of the absent presence of Jesus. Jesus is absent, "He is not here. Look, there is the place they laid him" (v. 6). If we can speak of his presence in spite of everything, it is only under the form of a promise: "He is going ahead of you to Galilee, just as he told you" (v. 7). This promise is very strong: it picks up the words of Jesus (Mark 14:28) to which the messenger adds, "as he told you," as if he wanted to insist on the certainty of the promise. Let's notice moreover that these are the last words of the last discourse of the Gospel. The Gospel that had begun with the sentence "as it was written . . ." (Mark 1:2) ends with "as he told you." To the question about the identity of Jesus has been added for the readers the question of locality: Where can we meet Jesus? On the one hand, the readers are thus invited to reread the past (the early Jesus) and, on the other hand, to hope and find their bearings to the future. Whereas the first dyad led readers to understand the identity of the risen Christ from his earthly existence, the second dyad leads them to look again at the temporal and topographic dimension. I agree with those authors who read verse 7 at a symbolic level—a nonexclusive reading. The

5. Y. Bourquin, *Marc, une théologie de la fragilité: Obscure clarté d'une narration*, Le monde de la Bible 55 (Geneva: Labor et Fides, 2005) 314.

terms used in these last verses ("Jesus of Nazareth / he goes before you / Galilee / you will see") refer to the body of the text of the Gospel. The meeting with the Christ will take place by rereading the Gospel and thus the life of Jesus as Mark has told it. This meeting with the Christ in all his glory still contains a provisional and incomplete aspect, because it will always keep the structure of the pre-Easter meetings in which are mixed the Passion and the resurrection. In the present, the reader who will keep in mind the future of the resurrected One must respect the past of the Passion.

In fact, can one still speak of a linear chronology when we speak of the Passion-resurrection unity and of an absent presence? By proposing a new form of existence of Jesus which goes beyond the limits of the thinkable—Jesus is simultaneously the one who suffers and the one who is resurrected; he is simultaneously the one who is present and the one that we must seek for—the narrator suggests that the veil, which covered Jesus in the Gospel from the eyes of those who were with him, still covers his identity from the eyes of those who will follow him after his death. The end is open and the responsibility to finish the narrative belongs to the reader. The "secret" still is not resolved, the meeting with the glory of the Christ has not yet taken place in the present.

Once Again: The Real Reader

At the end of the reading of the Gospel, we are in need of a real reader to continue. Many exegetes of Mark have understood the ending in this way. At the narrative and semantic dimensions of exegetical work, they explicitly add a pragmatic dimension. According to them, the understanding of the resurrection in Mark necessarily includes this call to action: "The power of Marks's gospel consists, not in the information that it communicates to the reader, but in what it challenges the reader to do."[6] This is not a little additional remark, invented by practical theologians or spiritual gurus. This "practical" dimension is part of the text. To the promise of Jesus (Mark 14:28) repeated by the messenger of God "to go to Galilee" (Mark 16:7) corresponds a human responsibility. In this sense Mark 16:8 functions as the "bridge" between two worlds, the one of the narrative and the one of the real reader.

6. P. J. Hartin, "The Role of the Women Disciples in Mark's Narrative," *Theologia Evangelica* 26 (1993) 91–102, esp. 99.

We have already seen that the first thing that is incumbent on the real reader is to reread the Gospel. The text offers him the source of the places of meeting with the Christ. The Gospel is the treasure that contains the roadmap leading to a meeting with the resurrected One. Thus, it is no exaggeration to say that the Gospel according to Mark is "saturated" with resurrection (Cuvillier) and that "the whole writing of the Gospel of Mark is guided by his understanding of the resurrection."[7] The post-Easter situation does not differ from the pre-Easter situation at the level of the facts; it is only at the level of the meaning that there is a change, but the readers are privileged by their knowledge of the Gospel.

Not only these passages that speak explicitly of the resurrection, but the *whole* of Mark's text breathes the presence of the resurrected One. The text of the Gospel is not only an *anticipation* of the resurrected One, but it also becomes a *realization* of the presence of Jesus. If anyone wants to see what the resurrection means in practice, they have to see how Jesus speaks and acts in the Gospel. Thus, the open ending discloses the narratives that go before it. We could have Mark 16:7 ("he goes ahead of you to *Galilee*") followed by the first summary of the Gospel in Mark 1:14b-15 ("Jesus came to *Galilee* . . ."). It is not enough to read the Gospel in its totality to better understand the end, because, in reverse, the finale from its side exactly allows a better understanding of the Gospel that precedes.

It is thus in life itself that the mystery of the passion and resurrection plays out. It was the case for those who met Jesus when he was alive, it was also the cases for all generations who have lived (before and after) and it is still true for us. The ultimate consequence for real readers, if they take the risk to answer positively the words of the messenger at the empty tomb, is to go farther and farther and perhaps even more quickly than foreseen into this mystery. If they begin to follow the model for life proposed by Jesus, they will not escape death, but they will learn to see how they will save their lives by losing them. The resurrection is never of the sole category of bliss. It is part of the mystery of life in which suffering and joy are mixed. Thus, the resurrection becomes a category more existential than temporal. For Mark, the resurrection is not an event that unfolds only after death, but in life.

7. C. Combet-Galland, "Qui roulera la peur? Finales d'évangile et figures de lecteur (à partir du chapitre 16 de l'évangile de Marc)," *Études Théologiques et Religieuses* 65 (1990) 171–89, esp. 105.

To Believe and Not to Believe

The theme of belief has already been broached on several occasions. The story of the empty tomb leads us there once again. The question that many ask is indeed obvious: "Is it true that Jesus was resurrected?" Like every other event in the Gospel, the story of the empty tomb must not be approached in isolation. It only makes sense when we consider it in the whole of the Gospel. The narrator has done everything to confront the reader with the identity of Jesus and from the beginning, he has endeavored to "believe" in this story. There does not exist, for example, any proof that the Kingdom of God begins at the moment in which Jesus casts out demons. There does not exist any proof that by healing a paralytic, Jesus is really the Son of God. There does not exist any proof to support the veracity of the Golgotha code ("to lose one's life to save it"). The readers only see resistance and misunderstanding about what Jesus does. If some readers decide in spite of everything to pursue reading to learn more about Jesus, they risk it despite good sense. They will have to first carry a negative judgment about the power of the adversaries and distance themselves from the lack of understanding of the disciples. They will likewise have to construct a new picture of God by reading the Gospel. But for those who have made this choice, the empty tomb narrative is the confirmation that God is really on the side of Jesus. For these readers, the empty tomb narrative is charged with meaning because it interacts with life. The way that Jesus assumed is necessary preparation for God to be able to raise him from the dead. And the resurrection is the confirmation of the life choices made by Jesus.

Thus, to believe or not to believe? What can that mean after contemporary readers read Mark's Gospel? Most important for Mark, it seems to me, is that we continue to hand on the narrative so that people are inspired by the life of Jesus to live like him. To live concretely thus is the true challenge for readers. For Mark, to believe in Jesus' resurrection is part of a bigger whole. In our days, people can receive this message in different ways. Those who lost the connection with the story of Jesus or who squarely turned away from God are numerous. Nevertheless, they often unconsciously (and sometimes involuntarily) relive Mark's story. They reply "yes" to it and choose to give their life for others. In acting in that way, they obviously "believe" because there is not the least bit of certainty that this is the option that makes the most sense in life. It is Mark's philosophy that people do not act in this way except when they believe. This way of life perfectly prolongs what Mark communicates to the readers, even if, in this case, these latter do not assign a religious dimension to their way of living. It is very possible that they see the narrative of the empty tomb as fantasy. Others are consciously in quest of meaning and religious content for their lives. Mark's narrative proposes to them through his protagonist Jesus a new picture of God. For the evangelist even, the story of Jesus' life is indistinguishable from the deep religious meaning with which it is involved: God reveals himself through his Son on the cross. For the readers who read the story in this way, the empty tomb is the sign that God is completely on Jesus' side. By considering Jesus' life as the presence of God in the world, they rightly interpret the narrative of the empty tomb as the ultimate expression that Jesus' life has not been lost but saved.

We mentioned at the beginning of the book how we can learn to treat the Gospel with different interpretations of the text. The passage of the empty tomb is a characteristic example of a text that will continue to divide people. From the historical point of view, it is indeed impossible to prove the thesis that God raised Jesus from the dead. But for Mark, this resurrection is not so much the object of disagreement between people. It only became that later. The Gospel's criterion for how to judge if someone is near Jesus' picture of God is to see if their way of life corresponds to the hermeneutic of Golgotha. People can really be near one another through the concrete way of living the Gospel, all the while having fundamentally divergent opinions about essential points of the faith. Mark's book thus stimulates dialogue.

For Further Reading

Combet-Galland, C. "Qui roulera la peur? Finales d'évangile et figures de lecteur? (à partir du chapitre 16 de l'évangile de Marc." *Etudes théologiques et religieuses* 65 (1990) 171–89.

Cuvillier, E. "La résurrection dans l'évangile de Marc ou: La finale courte . . . et puis avant?" In *Quand la Bible se raconte*, edited by D. Marguerat, 105–22. Lire la Bible 134. Paris: Cerf, 2003.

Danove, P. "The Characterization and Narrative Function of the Women at the Tomb (Mark 15, 40–41, 47; 16,1–8)." *Biblica* 77 (1996) 375–97.

Dettwiler, A. "Le mystère de la résurrection. Considérations théologiques à partir de Marc 16,1–8." In *Histoire et herméneutique*, edited by M. Rose, 139–50. Festschrift Gottfried Hammann; Histoire et Société 45. Geneva: Labor et Fides, 2002.

Focant, C. "Un silence qui fait parler (Mc 16,8)." In *New Testament Textual Criticism and Exegesis*, edited by A. Denaux, 79–96. Festschrift J. Delobel; Bibliotheca Ephemeridum Theologicarum Lovaniensium 161. Louvain: Peeters, 2002 =

Marc, un évangile étonnant: Recueil d'essais, 342–358. Bibliotheca Ephemeridum Theologicarum Lovaniensium 194. Louvain: Peeters, 2006.

Hartin, P. J. "The Role of the Women Disciples in Mark's Narrative." *Theologia Evangelica* 26 (1993) 91–102.

Heil, J. P. "The Progressive Narrative Pattern of Mark 14,3–16,8." *Biblica* 73 (1992) 331–58.

Hester, J. D. "Dramatic Inconclusion: Irony and the Narrative Rhetoric of the Ending of Mark." *Journal for the Study of the New Testament* 57 (1995) 61–86.

Lincoln, A. T. "The Promise and the Failure: Mark 16:7–8." *Journal of Biblical Literature* 108 (1989) 283–300.

Petersen, N. R. "When Is the End Not the End? Literary Reflections on the Ending of Mark's Gospel." *Interpretation* 34 (1980) 151–66.

Standaert, B. "Raconter la résurrection. Un paradoxe narrative." In *Resurrection in the New Testament*, edited by R. Bieringer, V. Koperski et B. Lataire, 73–91. Festschrift J. Lambrecht; Bibliotheca Ephemeridum Theologicarum Lovaniensium 156. Louvain: Peeters, 2002.

Williams, J. F. "Literary Approaches to the End of the Gospel of Mark." *Journal of the Evangelical Theological Society* 42 (1999) 21–35.

www.ingramcontent.com/pod-product-compliance
Lightning Source LLC
LaVergne TN
LVHW101320110826
845152LV00014B/153/J

* 9 7 8 1 4 9 8 2 2 2 1 9 8 *